The Secrets of SUCCESSFUL Public Relations

and image-making

Books in the series

The Secrets of
SUCCESSFUL
PUBLIC
RELATIONS

and image-making

Tony Greener

Heinemann Professional Publishing

Heinemann Professional Publishing Ltd
Halley Court, Jordan Hill, Oxford OX2 8EJ

OXFORD LONDON MELBOURNE AUCKLAND SINGAPORE
IBADAN NAIROBI GABORONE KINGSTON

First published 1990

British Library Cataloguing in Publication Data
Greener, Tony
The secrets of successful PR and image – making.
1. Public relations
I. Title   II. Series
659.2

ISBN 0 434 90696 4

Printed in Great Britain by
Billing & Sons Ltd, Worcester

Contents

Preface

Many people imagine that they know what PR is – and some of them are right. Many people imagine that they can 'do PR' just as well as a PR professional, or that they could if only they had the time. In this respect, only some of them are right. But most of them could have a good shot at understanding more about what PR involves – and that would benefit both them and the PR people who work with them.

As with many professional practices, PR has, consciously or otherwise, surrounded itself with jargon and mystique, has taken itself too seriously and has attempted to mature as a profession in record quick time. All these actions are perfectly understandable; everybody desires a modicum of security and a measure of respect in their working lives.

But, for the small businessperson at whom this book is aimed, these barriers are unhelpful. There is often a desire to know more about this high profile PR world. There is a desire to understand the workings of a PR consultant so that sensible commercial decisions can be taken based on an informed awareness of the issues involved. There is a need to understand how the media works before attempting to influence it. There is a need to understand how internal communications and external PR can complement – or hinder – each other. And there is a need to know how the general publicity and marketing effort of the business-person's company interacts with PR to form a more complete service.

Once more is known about these issues, more informed judgements can be taken. And it is this kind of straightforward information which this book sets out to provide.

It does not pretend to be a bible, or an exhaustive reference work or even a DIY manual. It simply sets out to give a brief look at the kind of PR practices which are relevant to the small businessperson. Inevitably, it will date because the profession is dating all the time. Inevitably, not all of it will be relevant to every reader.

Equally, some of it will help some readers to understand more about PR as it does, or can, relate to them. Some of it may provoke thoughts about how readers can use the information or act as a checklist for embarking upon PR exercises.

But if it proves readable and moderately useful, it will have done its job.

Tony Greener

1 What is public relations?

Ironically, public relations probably suffers from a worse press than almost any other profession. The art of presenting a positive message about themselves seems to elude many of the otherwise smart practitioners who use their skills to persuade the public to buy unwanted goods. This lack of clarity is not only ironical, it is also counterproductive for the PR industry itself because no self-respecting business of any size can afford to ignore some aspects of public relations.

Apart from anything else, there is a great deal of confusion over exactly what PR is. Most of us have heard of it. Some of us use it. Few of us really understand it. And yet, it's been around a long time – if under other names.

The first recorded application of the art dates from the time when Moses was standing on the shore of the Red Sea with his Public Relations Officer by his side, hundreds of Israelites looking to him for leadership and thousands of Egyptians bearing down upon them in chariots.

'What are we going to do now?' asked the PRO.

Moses thought for a while and then said, 'How's this? What about if I arrange it so that the sea divides leaving a dry causeway in the middle for us to walk over? Then, when the

Egyptians get here, the sea can roll back again and drown them all?'

The PRO thought about this long and hard and finally said, 'It'll never work. Tell you what though; if it does, I'll guarantee you a double page spread in the Old Testament.'

The actual coverage in the Old Testament is sixteen verses covering less than half a page, which just goes to show that PROs have always erred on the optimistic side in their forecasts of coverage, even when miracles are performed....

This book is designed to give an introduction to the more conventional and modern practice of public relations, and to present guidelines for the layperson setting out the ground rules, introducing the main activities which take place under the PR banner and addressing some of the pitfalls and advantages of the art.

It is specifically aimed at the small to medium sized business or organization and, wherever possible, the examples quoted are relevant to this area. In some instances, it happens that more graphic examples exist in larger businesses or the public sector. Where this is so, these examples are given for greater clarity.

The principles involved, however, do not differ in any way from one organization to another or from one PR practitioner to another. It is merely the method by which they are put into operation which might vary.

What is it?
First, what exactly is PR? – and why might you need it anyway?

There's still a popular misconception that PR is mainly the gin-and-tonic brigade, adept at 'whining-and-dining', spending other people's money with alarming freedom and generally having a high old time. Actually, it isn't like this: and if it ever was, it certainly isn't any longer.

Before we define it, let's try to establish *what it isn't*.

1 It isn't words or pictures about your organization that you have paid a newspaper, magazine, radio or TV station to carry. That's advertising.
2 It isn't brochures, leaflets, posters, labels, tickets, dispensers, counter displays or other similar literature. That's marketing, and, specifically, point-of-sale material.
3 It isn't the constant portrayal of a leading figure as being paramount in his or her field. That's self-aggrandizement.
4 It isn't a section of the Marketing Department which acts only as an obtainer of free coverage for your product range; although that may be a key part of its function.
5 It isn't a service to reserve private suites in the Savoy, book tables in Langans, order the coffee or drive the Chairman's children to the zoo. That's the role of either the secretary or the au pair, depending on the attitude of Mrs Chairman.
6 It isn't the automatic right to have your point of view recorded for posterity by a journalist or other influencer of the public. That's impossible.

Yet it can embody all these areas – and a great deal more besides. We'll explore the broad range of PR and publicity activities throughout this book.

Perhaps *what it is* can best be summed up in the sentence:

'The positive presentation of an organization to all its publics.'

In other words, controlling the way in which you present yourself – and are presented – in order to influence the way in which people think of you.

And the word 'publics' in a PR sense does not just mean the public or even external bodies; it also means employees, business suppliers, associates and partners, the media, trade networks, industry watchdogs and financial backers, as well as a whole host of influential groups of people known in the PR industry as 'Target Audiences'.

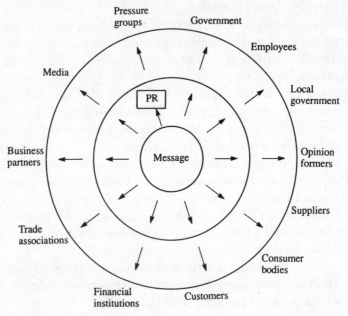

Figure 1   Target audiences

PR exists therefore to:

- build reputations of companies and organizations,
- build reputations of individuals as experts in their chosen field,
- increase awareness of products or services and of the organization which provides them,
- enhance credibility of a public position or a company's worth,
- mount a campaign aimed at achieving a specific objective.

In other words, PR aims to make people think more highly of you and your organization. And this aim can be carried out either in-house with your own staff or by using the services of a PR consultancy.

Two-way communication

PR is not simply a one-way flow of information; it has a two-way role as well. It can, for example, help to shape your organization by informing management of the expectations, opinions and concerns of these publics and explaining and advising upon consequent action. In this role, PR is firmly a management function, charged with the responsibility of managing an organization's reputation – shaping, protecting and promoting it.

It does this by a huge spread of activity – perhaps wider than most other professions. Press and media relations is the best known and, certainly one of the most important disciplines, but in reality any channel of communication is a PR opportunity.

A campaign, therefore, may include writing and publishing brochures, leaflets, posters and advertisements, lobbying national or local government, holding briefing sessions and presentations for pressure groups and influential individuals, embarking upon educational programmes (sometimes actually in schools or colleges), persuading third parties to write or comment favourably to lend support from quarters which are perceived to be impartial, arranging exhibitions and conferences, organizing visits to venues by important pressure groups and, almost inevitably, persuading the press and media to support the cause.

Some of these activities might have been undertaken in any organization (the advertising or the lobbying of local government, for example). But, taken as a whole, they require a PR co-ordinator to mould them into an effective expression of the case, to ensure consistency of message, accuracy of information and, above all, that the message is properly put across, received and understood.

One of my previous bosses (a notable captain of industry) defined, or redefined, the classic definition of the principle of communication.

'There are three main stages,' he said. 'First, you must define what you want to say and say it clearly and concisely. Then you must ensure that it has been understood by those to whom it has been communicated. Finally, you must ensure that the audience knows exactly what you want them to do as a result of your communication, and that must include a right of reply. Without these elements, you're wasting your time.'

These three cardinal rules (*to clarify, to express and to ensure understanding*) govern most that is beneficial in PR terms. They also ensure that thought must be given to the objective and how this is going to be achieved.

Accordingly, the objectives must be established in your own mind as a necessary precursor to the process of PR – just as it must to many other business activities.

Once the objectives have been agreed, the strategy of how they are to be attained must be devised and put into operation.

Finally, the degree of success must be evaluated so that future exercises start from a more informed base and so that any oversights or omissions can be rectified.

Put in this somewhat theoretical way, the whole task may sound dry and clinical – as any profession can be at times. The practice is very different, however (at least in my experience): never less than interesting, sometimes exciting, often fraught. The challenge of influencing people's thinking and of changing their minds remains fresh and absorbing even after many years in the business. A couple of examples may help to illustrate this.

The Great Dunlop Squash Racket
One good example of pro-active product PR is the launch of the Dunlop MAX 500G squash racket in the autumn of 1985. It was the latest in the Dunlop range of rackets – of which there were a dozen or so – and, consequently, it had

to be made to stand out from the rest as well as from the competition, especially to justify its premium pricing position.

All the usual advertising and point-of-sale activities were planned with a substantial launch budget. This was all fine as far as it went. However, it was important to address the large body of keen squash players (there are about two million players in the UK alone) who would not necessarily be exposed to this campaign. So we decided to mount a regional press launch, partly because local papers are a great place to sell consumer goods and partly because the specialist squash media is very restricted.

The problem here was that there was very little reason for regional newspapers to write about a new squash racket which had little local or national news interest. Somebody introduces new rackets every five minutes and they all look much the same – and play in much the same way as well – true 'Me,Too' products.

So, we decided to use the services of Dunlop Slazenger's best-known retained squash player, Jonah Barrington, to host a series of press launches at prestigious squash clubs throughout the UK – Canons in London, the Priory in Birmingham and the Village in Manchester. By this means we were able to invite literally hundreds of journalists all within a couple of hours' travel of these venues.

The evening began with a brief (five minutes) presentation on the background to the squash racket market so that the journalists were given the context in which the product was being launched and the strength of the Dunlop brand in that market (over 40 per cent, if memory serves).

The Squash Manager then described the properties of the MAX 500G and especially the benefits of the high technology design with its hollow, carbon fibre frame. He introduced a seven minute video – also featuring Jonah – illustrating these properties. After this, journalists had the opportunity to ask questions and discuss the main issues before Jonah gave one of his famous clinics.

In this, he talked very entertainingly about squash in general for about an hour, illustrating some of his points with a hapless, volunteer guinea pig player (who received a free racket for his pains). Then Jonah rounded off the evening with an exhibition match against a well-known local player, usually the unfortunate local squash club professional (Jonah likes to win his exhibition matches). A buffet gave further opportunity for discussion until the small hours.

The venues were packed at each session and the resulting regional coverage was very satisfactory. Much of the expenditure was being incurred in any case (the video was produced for clubs and retailers, for instance), but the entire cost was not more than a fraction of the launch advertising and promotional budgets. It was a drop in the ocean for a product which became by far the best selling squash racket in the UK within three months of launch.

The cost (which was less than £3,000 for each occasion) included all the press releases and photographs, invitations, hospitality and catering, hire of venues, Jonah's fee, travel and subsistence as well as a few free rackets. The evenings were enjoyable and successful and helped to forge stronger links with the clubs and the public as well as the press. It was a classic example of the product launch.

Shock! Horror! Drama!

The second example – and the other side of the coin is the responsive, defensive campaign aimed at damage limitation after events have gone badly wrong. As with most cases of this type, the PR specialists were called in only after it was too late to avert the damage altogether.

A well-known company had organized a national competition through its retail chain. On the day of the draw, the first correct entry taken at random out of a hat won a holiday villa, the second a car, and some twenty third places won less exotic prizes. During the draw there had, apparently, been some question over the order in which the winners were drawn, particularly as a wide geographical spread of winners would clearly result in greater regional publicity.

Some days after the draw, and after the results had been announced, one of the employees concerned left the company and promptly informed the editor of the local newspaper that irregularities had taken place in the allocation of prizes. What was worse was that he also tried to involve one of the major sensational Sunday papers, a medium which could easily have besmirched the good name of the company and done irreparable damage to its image.

Containing action was needed very quickly. It had to be totally convincing while preserving the integrity of the company in face of the possible shock, horror, drama which might break at any minute. As usual in these situations, we were hampered by the fact that we did not really know how much the informant knew, how much the newspapers knew or even what had really gone on at the draw. We had to play safe.

The first stage was to devise a holding statement in case the story was printed – a statement which upheld the company's integrity and professionalism while going some way towards admitting that there might be matters worth investigating. This statement was only to be used in a reactive mode, in case a journalist contacted us before we could ascertain the truth.

The next stage was to contact the main prize winners and ensure that they were happy with the way in which their prizes had been allocated. Before this, however, it was decided to award two first prizes and no second prize so that absolute fairness and justice could have been seen to be done.

Only then did the internal machine come into action: staff involved were interviewed, the truth finally extracted and appropriate action taken. At the same time, the security department investigated the background of the ex-employee who had created all the fuss and came up with some pretty damning circumstantial evidence.

In light of these developments, the press statement was updated just as the editor of the local paper (who was also the link into the Sunday scandal sheet) rang up to ask about the allegations. He was invited in for a full discussion and received and accepted the company's statement.

The resulting article he produced for his next issue was a model of responsible, objective reporting which reflected considerable credit on the company. The Sunday paper ignored the story altogether once it discovered that a happy ending was likely. Before the article appeared, all staff were fully briefed and considerable mileage was made both internally and externally of the company's integrity and generosity by awarding two first prizes instead of one.

And there, to all intents and purposes, it ended with all parties happy, damage limited to an extra first prize and considerable goodwill created in a number of prize-winning communities throughout the country. The ex-employee, faced with possible legal proceedings, vanished.

This incident, although greatly simplified and made anonymous in this narrative, is nevertheless a good example of the value of crisis management PR which can save a potentially explosive situation for a relatively modest outlay.

The standing of PR
So diverse is the field of PR that it defies a single label. Indeed the phrase 'Public Relations' itself is a misleading and hackneyed description which began to run out of credibility very quickly during the early 1980s. At that time, the vision of PR which many people had – and which some

may still have – was of the smarmy fixer glued to a gin and tonic, the Sloane whose need to work was debatable and who thought 'it would be fun to go into PR' or the pseudo-hack not talented enough to be a proper journalist, or even (much more likely) an improper one.

PR undoubtedly suffered because of the apparent light-weight nature of its business. Perhaps, it also suffered because a number of less than ethical elements were attracted to the fast buck which could be made, especially in consultancies – not an occurrence unique to PR....

The depth of suspicion about the label is still consider-able. I once knew a consultant chemical pathologist whom I was helping in the preparation and delivery of a paper to be given at an international conference of highly eminent medics in Brazil. 'You know,' he said one night after we had rewritten his slides and script for the umpteenth time, 'I never used to think much of PR people.' It's still all too common an outlook.

As with most professions, public relations has its govern-ing bodies although the major one, the Institute of Public Relations (IPR), probably wields over its members only a fraction of the power developed over the years by, say, the Law Society. However, it performs useful work in training, in advising and in laying down codes of practice for its members. So does the Public Relations Consultants Asso-ciation (PRCA), to which most reputable PR consultancies belong. These two bodies in particular have been respons-ible for much of the codifying of practice within the business and have greatly helped the inevitable growth pains over the last two decades.

The guises under which PR operates

Partly as a result of the backlash against the PR label, and partly for a complex variety of reasons, there arose a proliferation of names for in-house employees who carried out work of a PR nature. This has led to a most confusing number of titles for thousands of people doing very similar work.

The public sector, for example, perceived the need for some form of PR service during the early 1970s, although a few areas, notably in central government and nationalized industry, had been using the facility for a long time before that, albeit in a low key way. What especially gave impetus to the rapid acquisition of PR expertise was the greater openness and accountability of the public sector (one of the more practical and enduring outcomes of the 1960s protest movements) together with the far reaching changes to local government which first emerged around 1974.

In this, relatively, socialist climate of opinion in the late 1960s and early 1970s, however, – perhaps the only true one ever to have been seen in the UK – any practice which smacked of capitalist exploitation was ostensibly taboo in official circles. This was especially so at a time when private enterprise was much less fashionable than it is now, when employment was relatively full and when the spectre of Rachmann and Poulson haunted those in authority.

Terms such as 'PR', 'advertising', and 'publicity', while not exactly dirty words, were not exactly trusted by those still grappling with the problems of implementing the liberal, alternative dreams of the 1960s in a society whose fabric was being increasingly torn by economic ills, radical reform and industrial strife.

Consequently, employers in local government, education and health authorities and quangos circumvented the difficulty of jumping on the bandwagon of greater communication and openness without compromising their ideals by calling the PR practitioners it was busily recruiting by some other name.

'Information Officer' was one which was, and still is, greatly favoured by universities, colleges and some of the public utilities.

Of the other commonly found terms, 'Communications' became burdened with yet another meaning and one which is still confusing to many who expect it to represent aspects of technology or postal services. 'External Relations' or 'External Affairs' acquired favour in both private and public sector organizations which had difficulty with 'PR' and restrict themselves to externally targeted work. 'Employee Relations' grew in the 1970s and early 1980s when that responsibility quite often found itself transferred to the professional communicators in PR – often to the despair of the Personnel Department.

Those with vision in the early and mid-1970s saw that PR – in whatever guise – would become an indispensable part of the 'Marketing Mix', that grandiose title which describes a rag-bag of duties from pricing to market research to advertising.

Thus, as enterprise and marketing began to regain credibility (a process heavily boosted by the Conservative Party's appointment of Saatchi & Saatchi to help it improve its image and win elections) so the proliferation of titles crept into the private sector as well. Companies with the need for strong sales support pushed PR people into marketing departments, sometimes as 'Product Affairs' staff, or simply as 'Publicity' people.

In order to distinguish the market support role from the broader business-wide role, therefore, 'Corporate Affairs' or 'Corporate Relations' titles began to appear and are now the accepted label in a number of large organizations.

Latterly, something of a compromise has been reached with the adoption of yet another variation: 'Public Affairs'. This a friend of mine once somewhat sourly remarked was all too appropriate for the role. 'They can't do anything decently in private,' he observed. 'They've even got to make a public drama out of their sex lives.' It was probably just sour grapes.

Whatever it's called, PR is here to stay and to be used and the number of organizations with an awareness and appreciation of what it has to offer increases every day.

Who needs it?

All organizations, private or public, who have a need to communicate their point of view convincingly to any audience need some sort of PR service.

But isn't communicating with other people or entities largely common sense? Yes, it is; but there are also many different ways of applying that sense and a large number of professional techniques involved in the expression of what you want to say. This is where PR is a practical combination of the best method and the best discipline to achieve your objectives.

It may well be that the relatively new emergence of this profession (twenty years ago it was far less widespread) is partly a process of bringing a wide variety of traditional communications needs and skills under one umbrella. It may also be that this process has impinged upon several other areas of communication while overlaying them with a veneer of skills and respectability, some of it imported from the US.

There are three main reasons why an organization needs a PR service of one form or another:

1 It is *extremely cost effective* in comparison to other methods of communicating and publicizing a message. An advertising campaign for a new product, for example, can quite easily cost in the region of £500,000 even without TV exposure. A PR campaign to promote the same product is quite feasible for 10 per cent of that cost. There won't be quite the same control over what is said, or where and when but this is often more than compensated for by the second factor.

2 The *impartial opinion*. By having your new product reviewed in the press and media, the public is reassured

that an independent, third party observer has tested it, understands it and is reasonably sure that it represents fair value for money. No advertisement can achieve that effect because it is always perceived – perhaps subconsciously – as paid for space or air-time which carries a hard sell message or even propaganda. Perhaps surprisingly, the general public still believes what it reads in the papers to a very high degree.

3 PR has become an *essential tool* in the overall process of business growth. It is now an integral part of the combination of disciplines which go to make up any properly structured organization, either private or public. Operating across its three classic areas of product, business and internal affairs, it provides a service complementary to the overall objectives of growth and profitability by interlocking with marketing, sales, personnel, manufacturing, purchasing, finance, engineering, business planning and all the other elements of a modern, integrated business structure. Indeed, in many respects, it cuts across all these in a way in which few other operations are able to do and, in some structures, the PR Director is closer to the Chairman or Chief Executive than any comparable director.

As a profession, PR is still very much in its formative years. It does not yet have the seniority or the respect afforded to other professions, such as law and accountancy, nor is it necessarily ever going to achieve this. What it does have is a power to change people's minds, sometimes in an open and direct fashion, sometimes in an altogether more subtle and delicate way, more akin to the intrigues of an Italian Renaissance court than to the hurly-burly of modern business. Jack of all skills and master of none, except the power of expression, it has an enduring and increasing role in modern society.

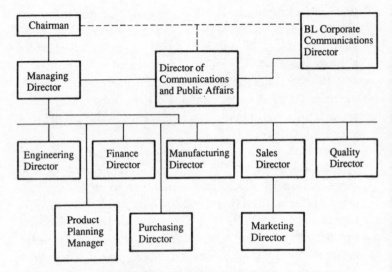

Figure 2   Land Rover Ltd Organization chart 1981–2

Applying PR in practice

All this theory is all very well but the reason you've bought this book is to find out how to conduct successful PR activity as an integral part of your overall business. By now, you may be feeling that it's about time you got your teeth into something concrete. Very well then. The rest of the book is geared to the problems and opportunities of the PR world.

It covers most of the areas in which you'll need to operate and provides an introduction to the kind of services that you may need to call upon to bolster your efforts. For, although a great deal of PR is common sense, hard work and the application of basic principles (just like any other skill) there are a number of specialized areas in which you would do well to take the advice, if not the full-time services, of a professional. Parliamentary and financial affairs, for example, are not dealt with in any great detail here, largely because they are so specialized that it is usually necessary to retain a professional to conduct this aspect of the PR business for you.

What this book sets out to do is to lay out the foundation skills necessary if you want to conduct your own PR activity, even to a limited extent. We discuss the rudiments of relations with the press and media, your local community and your own employees, and indicate the nature and value of sponsorship, an activity which often runs hand in hand with a PR programme. We also touch on the advantages and pitfalls of retaining a PR consultancy to do all or part of the job for you. If you decide to go this route, therefore, you will be more aware of what you want from the service, how you should be briefing the consultancy, what you should be paying and what you ought to be getting in return.

This book does not pretend to be a bible, or even an exhaustive list of PR skills. Some aspects of the trade are deliberately omitted as being unnecessary detail at this stage. It merely sets out one approach to realizing the potential which exists for most literate business people who wish, and need, to raise the profile, and thereby the standing, of their organizations.

Before we go into detail, therefore, here is a brief description of the main types of PR operation to help you to decide in which areas you need to concentrate your effort.

Product PR
This is the most common and traditional aspect of PR work: the promotion of the product, brand or service, usually through the press and media. It involves persuading journalists to write about a product or service, preferably in a positive way but, at least, to write about them. This brings the subject to the notice of the customer without the prohibitive costs of advertising while, at the same time, imbuing it with the benefit of an informed third opinion.

Product PR is obviously very useful to launch a new product when a consistently high level of visibility is required (this is dealt with more fully in Chapter 3). It is also used, however, to keep the product in front of the public. Most of the cars which appear in fictional programmes on TV and in cinema films, for example, are placed there after much hard work from the PR department of the car companies, invariably without charge and, it has been rumoured, sometimes with backhanders to ensure selection ahead of the competition.

More people are employed in product PR than in any other form of the art and it remains the staple diet of most PR consultancies, largely because it is the most frequently required service, especially by small and medium sized companies.

To many PR practitioners – and especially consultancies – it is also the most tedious aspect of the business and often tends, therefore, to be relegated to the more junior staff whose enthusiasm to ring up journalists and sell product stories remains as yet undimmed. Be that as it may, the skill to pull down the coverage is still the one which is most in demand from the majority of clients.

Business PR

Often a more subtle approach, business PR involves creating the impression that the company from which the customer is buying his product or service is a fundamentally sound one with good track records and potential in such areas as growth, profitability, stability and so on. Often used to reinforce the product PR effort, it can contribute greatly to the confidence a public has in an operation.

A great deal of the hype with which the Austin Metro was launched in 1980, for instance, was built up on the basis of the new Birmingham factory with its revolutionary automated equipment and advanced robotics. In the mind of the public, a company that was so progressive had to be producing an advanced car and, for its time, the Metro was just that.

Although often dealing with the financial side of the business, especially results, performance and investment, business PR is not strictly speaking financial PR in that it is aimed more at the customer, the supplier, the trade network, the public and, perhaps, specific industry bodies, than at the City and financial institutions. Nevertheless, the two are very close and many campaigns can be aimed at both sets of audiences with only minor changes.

The communication of the employee relations and industrial relations issues, which from time to time haunt our newspapers, are also an important part of the business PR remit, fortunately less so now than during the unrest of the 1960s, 1970s and early 1980s.

Financial PR
A highly skilled branch of the discipline, financial PR requires a thorough knowledge of the workings of the City with its myriad financial institutions, rules and regulations, particular habits and requirements of investors and analysts and the intricacies of the Stock Exchange. So tightly focused is it that the majority of financial PR practitioners make a very comfortable living by specializing in this and nothing else. For several years now, there has been a dearth of good financial PR talent and you will find this is fully reflected in the fees of a financial PR consultant.

Unless you are quoted on the full Stock Exchange, are threatened by an unwelcome takeover, wish to take over somebody else against their wishes, have a burning need to raise cash without going through the usual channels or wish to be listed on the USM, financial PR is not an area to get into. Consequently, this book doesn't deal with it in any great detail although it is partly covered in Chapter 9 which deals with the whole question of employing a consultancy.

Political PR
This is another highly specialized field which concerns itself

very largely with Parliamentary lobbying in which activity there has been a noticeable increase over the last ten years. Usually run by ex-politicians or ex-civil servants, it is not a discipline which has too much in common with mainstream PR and will not be dealt with in these pages.

The lobbying of local government and other public bodies is, however, a different kettle of fish altogether and is covered as part of the business PR range of activities. In particular, local government relations are addressed in Chapter 6.

Internal PR

This, one of the most important areas in which anyone can operate, was for many years a personnel responsibility and, in many organizations, still is. However, it is not coincidence that one of the first actions taken by Sir Michael Edwardes when he assumed the chairmanship of strike-torn British Leyland in 1978 was to switch responsibility for employee communications from the Personnel Department to the Public Relations Department.

Since employees are in many ways the most difficult of all audiences with whom to communicate, it follows that those practitioners who are best at communicating need to be heavily involved. The subject is discussed in detail in Chapter 8.

2 Media relations

The most important route through which much PR effort is directed is the media. Although the word is sometimes used to define only the more modern methods of broadcast communications such as TV and radio, to many PR people it means the whole area in which journalists work: newspapers and magazines as well as free sheets, house newspapers and the multiplicity of periodicals.

To approach the challenge of persuading a section of the media to report your point of view, you need to do your homework. First of all you need a 'story'. Nobody is going to write a glowing report of your latest product or service just to keep you in business unless it has an inherent news value or interest. Stories, in journalist parlance, are chunks of information which will appeal to the readership, attract advertisers, bring a deserving cause, a scandal or a social issue to the notice of the reading public, improve circulation figures or otherwise benefit the community.

In very few cases does this definition meet your requirements so, before trying to create your story, it is as well to establish exactly what you are trying to do with whom. Only once you've done so can you embark upon a media relations exercise with a reasonable chance of success.

In order to do this, you first of all need to know something about the media. If you do not it's impossible to target your story to the most likely outlets and so you'll simply waste a great deal of time and money for no good purpose. Targeted PR (a buzz term among PR consultants) means just that: the identification of the kind of media which:

1 reaches your desired audience and
2 might be amenable to printing your story.

Clearly, if a publication fails to satisfy either of those requirements, and especially the first, then you're aiming wide of the mark.

So, what kinds of media channels are there in the UK from which to choose?

And, having chosen them, how do you go about persuading them to print your story?

An answer to the second part occupies Chapter 3 but here we look briefly at some of the more important and influential kinds of media and at the type of people with whom you may have dealings during the course of your media relations programme.

The newspaper

This is a fairly obvious place to start: almost the oldest established and most traditional of the forms of publication that society enjoys.

Newspapers break down into two basic categories: the nationals and the locals.

The nationals

Here are all the famous old names redolent of printers' ink and hot metal – although nowadays they're nearly all produced on computers. Nevertheless, there's still something splendidly traditional about the idiosyncratically coloured paper on which the *Financial Times* is printed, or the ornate masthead of the *Daily Telegraph*, or the small ads in the *Times*.

Most newspapers tend to be conservative in their outlook; editors and reporters may be as radical as they like in some ways, but the companies for whom they write dislike change – when it happens to them – just as much as anyone else and perhaps even more than most.

Generally speaking, nationals aren't much good to small businesspeople. Their advertising rates are very high, their editorial space is limited and they usually need stories with wider reader appeal and greater national significance than the fact that you've just opened a new dry cleaning shop in Broadstairs. In any case, most small businesses are more interested in the local area and national newspapers are not the ideal media to reach this market.

Where they are excellent is in helping to create a climate of opinion in which to achieve a set objective. They also excel in drawing the attention of a large body of readers to a situation with national implications.

If, for instance, you've perfected a cure for cancer which the NHS won't implement because it's too expensive, you can – and should – use the pages of anything you can find to draw attention to the fact. Not only will this probably awaken social conscience on a national scale; it is also likely to result in action of some kind. At best, the government will subsidize the product; at worst, you'll have created awareness in a thriving private market and hope for (and demand from) thousands of people.

But that's a big, emotive issue guaranteed to command national attention. If you are associated with a pressure group which feels that too many hedgerows are being grubbed out in your local area, you'll have to demonstrate the despoiling of the countryside on a national scale – or a test case in an area of national significance such as the Lake

District – before you get half the column space that the cancer cure would automatically command.

If you cannot claim a national interest in your story, then the chances are that the national paper will simply ignore you.

The big exception is the world of business. You may only run a dry cleaners in Broadstairs, but, if you try to take over Grand Met, you'll soon find a very healthy level of interest in your business operations. If, as might be likely, you get into financial difficulties, you'll probably find this attention positively overwhelming.

All the media loves a disaster story – although all of them might not admit it – because that's what many ghoulish humans like to read, so it's good for circulation figures and, in turn, for advertising revenue, where newspapers make their real money.

Only when you're committed to escalating an issue do you begin to earn the interest of the big boys in Fleet Street: close down a plant, refuse to negotiate with the unions or pay compensation and you'll receive attention – from many quarters. Declare yourself bankrupt and blame it on the government's latest legislation and you might make the back page. (Not the front; that's reserved for bad news, Royal weddings and TV soap stars.)

So, what is there to aim at in the national press? And which one might be right for one of your bigger stories?

The three groups
Britain's national daily newspapers fall naturally into three major groups – the qualities, the middle-of-the-road and the popular tabloids. With a few modifications, the Sunday papers can also be made to conform to these categories. However, it should be stressed that this is only a convenient and simplistic division of the media.

The qualities

These are the traditional heavyweights which have contributed greatly to the development of British society over the last 200 years.

The Times (circulation 471,500) is perhaps the best known of all the British – and maybe even the world's – newspapers. It was known to Victorian readers as 'The Thunderer' on account of its vigorous support for causes ranging from the conduct of the Crimean War to the Irish Home Rule question. It has always revelled in, and sometimes relaxed in, its reputation as one of the foremost opinion formers on matters of political, religious, economic, social and military moment. Characters in Dornford Yates' novels 'raise quizzical eyebrows from the Personal Column of the *Times*' although they never dreamed of an occupation as vulgar as buying or selling anything.

Nowadays, although no longer *the* paper, the *Times* remains one of the best in terms of objective analysis and opinion, both of news stories and of current trends, although there is an impression that these are conveyed mainly to the converted and the retired.

The Daily Telegraph (circulation 1,156,300) is the best seller of the qualities and regarded – especially by its detractors – as the bourgeois bugle. Unashamedly middle class values go hand-in-hand with moderation and reason and its excellent sports and business pages probably do much to keep its circulation in the rarefied atmosphere over one million.

More approachable than the *Times*, it was established much later (in 1855 as opposed to 1785) but can still claim a long pedigree. For PR consumer stories it is a slightly better bet because it is more approachable and devotes marginally more space to smaller domestic stories. Nevertheless, it will still need to be convinced of the national relevance of a new product or service before running a story.

The Guardian (circulation 524,300) is older than the *Daily Telegraph*, having been founded in 1821 as the *Manchester Guardian* and has traditionally appealed to the more liberal – or 'free thinking' – elements of the quality readership. It is also the paper beloved of some academics and most educationalists, teachers and creative or media readers. Yet curiously, in light of its reputation, it is only comparatively recently that it ceased to eschew a racing column on moral grounds. Any story with a social theme stands quite a good chance of being printed in the *Guardian* especially if it champions the underdog in his struggle against bureaucracy.

The Business Bible is the *Financial Times* (circulation 251,600) most of which is fairly incomprehensible to those who do not have some grasp of, or interest in, business and the mysterious cult of money making. Nor is it the paper for the small private investor who is unlikely to be able to find the listing of his shares among the many pages of financial columns which confront him. Indeed, the small investor is better off reading the other qualities; the FT is principally a financiers' and companies' paper with comparatively few copies being bought by private individuals.

A must for takeover, investment or company results stories, and remarkably good for appointments, it is skimpy in its coverage of news which doesn't affect business and pretty well a dead loss for the sporting reader. Among the purse holders of financial institutions, however, it is hugely influential and many copies may be seen on the morning trains into the City. Moreover, it is likely to run business-based stories that are too specialized for the other quality papers.

The Independent (circulation 375,000) is the baby of this group, having been founded in 1986. Its intention was to create a truly independent forum for debating current issues, one which took no account of party politics or entrenched, traditional values.

To a certain extent, it has begun to achieve this. By attracting some of the best journalists from other papers, it quickly acquired a reputation for excellent writing. Some doubts were expressed about its financial viability for a while – perhaps inevitably for such a bold initiative. These now seem to have blown over and the *Independent* looks set to join the establishment, however loudly it proclaims that it won't.

The middle-of-the-road papers

These are difficult to categorize being caught, somewhat uneasily, between the qualities and the out and out pops. Coincidentally, the two best known, the *Daily Express* (circulation 1,855,600) and the *Daily Mail* (circulation 1,801,300) were both founded within four years at the turn of the century and have more or less kept pace with each other ever since.

They were recently (1986) joined by *Today*, which has the unusual distinction of being published seven days a week and made history by being the first daily newspaper in the country to run daily colour pages. At first, the colour reproduction wasn't very successful but it has improved considerably and, with the newspaper surviving a difficult first year, there is no reason to think that it will not, in time, join the *Express* and the *Mail* in the big circulation league.

All three papers differ from the qualities by carrying shorter articles and concentrating on a more newsy, lighter approach to their material. Although there are features about serious issues such as the destruction of the Brazilian rain forests, much of the news tends to be concentrated in half minute reading bursts in much the same way as TV advertising is constructed. There are only a couple of brief pages of City news and a good many snippets of unusual or off-beat information on a large number of news pages.

For the product story, these papers are often more use to the PR world than the qualities, especially as they often take seriously their championship of consumer rights. Their ability to accept copy is, however, strictly limited and even the best of their correspondents are constantly competing for space so that the cardinal rule of having a good story to tell assumes even greater importance.

The popular tabloids

Finally, there are the 'pops', the papers that have made a success of persuading their readers to laugh at themselves. Between them, the big three, the *Daily Mirror* (circulation 3,049,000), *The Sun* (circulation 4,062,000) and *The Star* (circulation 1,421,000), reflect the reading habits of over a third of the population of the UK.

Of these, the *Mirror* has almost always – since its foundation in 1903 – been the voice of the left wing in general and the Labour Party in particular. It is probably less influential than it used to be, partly because it was forced into a ruthless circulation war by the more right wing *Sun* when that paper rose above the horizon during the 1960s. It is also notoriously difficult to influence and apart from the really big story of national political or social importance, probably best left alone by budding PR operators.

The Sun, which took the slightly grubby attitude which had been the *Mirror's* hallmark and turned it into unrelenting salaciousness with the strategic introduction of 'Page Three' girls, now claims the biggest circulation of any paper in the country. It is extremely professional in its marketing and uses every trick in the sales promotions book to retain the number one spot. With that sort of success, it can quite happily bear the brunt of Jasper Carrott's *Sun* Readers jokes; indeed, it probably promotes them as a sure way of maintaining circulation.

The Star is a rather pale imitation of the *Sun* relying heavily on sleaze, sensation, colour girls, Starbirds, bingo and more sleaze in order to titillate its readership. Since nearly 1.5 million people think it's worth 20p every day, its commercial success is assured but its editorial standards are seldom taken seriously – sometimes possibly even by those who write its columns.

No one should imagine that the pops are less professional in their outlook than the other papers. Part of the *Sun's* great success is its clever editorial policy. You'll be hard put to find a sentence longer than fourteen words and extremely hard put to find a word of more than three syllables. Whatever else they may be, the journalists on this paper are craftsmen, wordsmiths who know exactly what their readers want and how they want to read it. In their own way, they're every bit as skilled as the leader writers of the *Times* and their success in recent years bears this out.

Outside these groups, there are three other national papers: the *Morning Star, The Sporting Life* and the *Racing Post*. Unless you sell horses or horse meat, or are a compulsive gambler, you can safely ignore the last two. The *Morning Star*, founded in the dark days of the class struggle in 1930 as the voice of the British Communist Party, hasn't had an easy struggle itself, especially during the affluent 1980s, and has had to be rescued from bankruptcy on a number of occasions. Its current circulation is listed at 28,000, but there is a widespread belief in the newspaper world that this figure includes a significant number of copies destined for other communist parties abroad.

If you haven't read it since you were a student, it hasn't changed much; it's best summed up perhaps by its deathless coverage of the Royal wedding between Princess Anne and Captain Mark Phillips which went along the lines of: 'Traffic in the West End of London was disrupted yesterday owing to the marriage in Westminster of Anne Windsor and Mark Phillips.' Probably the shortest account of a State occasion ever but quite easy to write if you don't acknowledge the Royal family. Of course, the Royal family may not acknowledge the *Morning Star* either.

Finally, there's *The Sport*, spawned by the *Sunday Sport* and launched early in 1989. The editorial – of which there isn't much – is a marvellous tongue in cheek parody of tabloid style: 'White Mice in Sex Orgy', 'Bonking Brits in Benidorm'. (At least, I hope it's parody.) All the stories are either sex scandals or particularly gory murders. For press releases it's a dead loss – it's not much better for sport, incidentally – but you might find it responds to a promotion, especially if you've got a big prize to give away.

The Sundays
The Sundays are hugely influential, partly because they take advantage of the greater leisure time available to most readers on Sundays and partly because they take great care to publish fresh information, not just rehash a version of the week's news. Their features and reviews are highly regarded by PR operators and their investigative journalism is second to none, having rocked many boats over the years – from Rachmann to Thalidomide.

The list of quality Sundays is headed by the *Sunday Times* (circulation 1,150,000) which helped to launch the face of the 1960s by introducing the first free colour supplement in 1962. Its new technology section, called Innovation, and its new products pages are in great demand by all self-respecting PR operators and some of its journalists are the best in the English language.

Making modest but steady progress over the last few years is the *Sunday Telegraph* (circulation 678,250) which is regarded as being rather more right wing than the *Daily Telegraph* and has tended to specialize in City pages. News coverage is deliberately confined to a small number of stories, usually exclusive to the paper and written in considerable detail. It is not so highly coveted by product PR operators, but its business and financial coverage is constantly attracting extra PR attention.

The Observer (circulation 778,200) was, for some time, the major rival to the *Sunday Times*, but has experienced steadily declining sales throughout much of the 1970s and 1980s and has now had to admit the *Sunday Telegraph* as a comparable rival. A good colour section maintains a strong interest in changing fashions and is beloved of all good product PR people.

The middle ground papers still centre around the *Sunday Express* (circulation 2,375,000) which combines all its sections into one volume, unlike the numerous different sections of, say, the *Sunday Times*. Like most Sundays, its sports coverage is extensive although its news and feature content is restricted to short, readable snippets of fairly popular news. A relatively new rival in this sector is *The Mail on Sunday* (circulation 617,000) which boasts a good colour section and an editorial style very similar to the *Daily Mail*. It champions causes and opinions quite strongly with professional journalism and is set to improve its position in the Sundays' circulation league.

The popular section of the Sunday reading market is a huge one as the circulations of the big three demonstrate. The *Sunday Mirror* (circulation 3,053,000), *The People* (circulation 3,055,000) and The *News of the World* (circulation 4,850,000) testify to the Sunday reading habits of roughly half the population of the UK. They have achieved this success through a combination of exhaustive sports coverage, cheerful scandal and healthy vulgarity.

They are difficult targets for PR efforts because they usually want to print exactly what the PR operator doesn't want them to print. Bad news, especially of the salacious variety, is their meat and drink and they are best ignored by the would-be PR man – especially one who has something to hide.

In the same vein, you will find it difficult to extract from any of your friends or acquaintances an objective opinion of *Sunday Sport* because no one will admit to reading it. This could also be the reason why there are no official circulation figures registered for it. It is probably only of value if you sell outsize bras.

The locals

Gratifying though it undoubtedly is to see the name of your business in one of the national papers, seeing it in a local paper is far more use to most small companies. It is also considerably easier to achieve by PR methods. If you're looking for a new home or car, a secondhand Wendy House or a garden shrub, you're much more likely to be reading your local paper than the *Times*.

People read local papers far more thoroughly than nationals, too, mainly because a good deal of what they see is familiar; it's happening not to Mr Gorbachev but to Billy down the road who's been done for drunken driving again.

They also study adverts much more thoroughly because the chances are they know most of the shops or advertisers and that's reassuring when contemplating parting with money.

Consequently, the local paper is often far more use to you than the national press. And it's usually easier to get your story accepted and even to be able to influence the way in which it's written up – something that is harder to achieve at national level.

Local papers tend to be either daily – usually in cities – or weekly – in more rural areas. They're often the product of many years of takeovers and mergers and so they have a number of issues based in different centres to cover an area roughly the size of a county.

In my area, for example, the *Sussex Express*, merged with the *County Herald* at some point in its 150 year history and now runs eight main editions based in Lewes, Heathfield, Uckfield, Rye, Battle, Hailsham, Newhaven and Peacehaven. The central sections of the paper will be common to all eight issues, but the outside pages – those containing local news and sport – will be personalized to each area.

And, in order to make sure that readers know they're buying a paper written specially for their area, they aren't called the *Sussex Express*; they're called the *Lewes Express*, the *Heathfield Express*, and so on. You can buy advertising for one or more issues and you can get a story accepted on the same basis – simply by contacting your nearest branch office. The paper itself then cleverly packages its content so that you gain coverage in all the regional issues as though you were indigenous to each one. Not a bad system with which to cover a number of small county towns which, between them, contain a great deal of buying power.

The big regional dailies follow the same kind of format with considerable success. The *Birmingham Evening Mail*, for example, with a circulation of around 300,000, has satellite editions for Dudley and Sandwell, called the *Dudley Mail* and the *Sandwell Mail* but taking most of their content and advertising from the *Birmingham Mail* and carrying stories relevant to Dudley or Sandwell on the front page.

In my days on the *Reading Evening Post*, I was introduced to the mysteries of increasing and sustaining circulation, which is just as important to a newspaper as your turnover figures are to you. My boss told me to judge a local paper by its front page layout. If it contained a headline reference to at least one local place name above the fold (where it could easily be read on the newsagent's counter) then it was likely to be well run and enjoying a healthy circulation.

Free sheets

Relying solely on advertising revenue to keep going, free sheets first made their appearance in the early 1970s and have gone from strength to strength ever since. There are even a few cases of them forcing conventional local papers out of business. Now that most parts of the country are well served by free sheets, the boom is slowing down. This is excellent news both for the reader and the advertiser. Rates were held low for a long time in order to get into the local advertising market, although there are now signs among the better established free sheets that they're flexing their muscles and increasing their prices.

The bad news for PR operators is that few free sheets pay much attention to the editorial section; some shun it altogether – perhaps as a frivolous and non-profit making aspect of publishing – while those who do carry editorial tend to pay it lip service rather than do the job properly.

Very often, stories are restricted to précis of pieces sent in to the editor/proprietor and lumped together on the first few pages. Few, if any, free sheets have the luxury of an editor who does nothing but gather news, write it and edit it. Usually, the owners or managers do this in their spare time having spent most effort attracting the advertising revenue. Indeed, if they did not observe this priority, the paper would be very shortlived.

Nevertheless, free sheets need to be influenced because of the impressive circulation they command and because of their high level of readership. As a rough guide, most conventional papers are read by 2.5–3 times the number of people who buy them. This is known as a 'readership' figure. Most free sheets probably have a readership figure of 3–4 times their circulation, and are particularly influential as local centres of information exchange. If you can get into them, then do so; it will prove a good investment of time and effort.

Sometimes, across all forms of newspaper, there is an unofficial agreement that, in order to achieve editorial mention, you need to advertise with the publication first. This is strictly frowned upon by all quarters of the newspaper business and you'll never find anyone who'll admit to operating such a system – which only makes its existence the more mysterious.

After that very brief look at the newspapers on sale at most newsagents, we must look at a highly influential sector of the media which may not be on sale to the general public at all, but which can greatly assist in creating an image of respectability and success for your business.

The periodicals

There are two major categories here: magazines on sale to the general public, the consumer, whether by subscription or over the counter; and magazines, usually available on subscription only, aimed solely at the trade in which your business operates.

The consumer magazine

This group again subdivides into two: the specialist interest magazine (such as *The Bookseller*) and the lifestyle magazine, such as *Cosmopolitan*.

The specialist interest magazine is one of the best routes into the serious purchasers of your product, those who really shop around and examine the market background to ensure that they are buying the best product for their purposes and achieving the best value for money.

Car magazines, for example, are read by those who really want to know the details not only of the model they're thinking about buying but also about the car world in general. Some are bought by those who want a Ferrari but end up with an Escort. The majority of car buyers use local newspapers as well as – or instead of – car magazines.

Likewise, most categories of consumer goods have their own, sometimes extensive, media. There are, for example, literally hundreds of computer magazines with titles appearing and disappearing every month. There is a good, short-term market for publishers in following the latest fad; therefore short-term magazines have a meteoric existence if they're devoted to fashions such as skateboards or CB radio.

Lifestyle consumer magazines are very often not too specific about the range of topics they cover and this applies, for example, to several of the women's magazines and the rural periodicals, such as *Country Life* and the *Field*. Here are publications which have almost become an institution and are the more valuable for PR purposes as a result. They are trusted, traditional and believed. And, equally important, they enjoy long 'shelf lives', hanging around in doctors' and dentists' waiting rooms for months or even years after they have first appeared.

Even when products or services have a specialist media devoted effectively to their generic (unbranded) promotion, it is always worth examining and using the vertical media, that is, the broader interest publications which your buyer might also read.

So, although a Range Rover buyer might read *Car*, he might also read *Country Life*. A CD collector will read *Which CD* but is also in the market for skiing holidays and home computers. He is, therefore, likely to read a whole series of lifestyle magazines which may range from the *Face* to *Defence News*. A tennis player may read *Tennis World* but also *Fitness* magazine.

Therefore it's worth looking at – or commissioning – research into exactly who is buying your product, and who might like to, before trying to influence both the sector and the industry media. Following from this, it clearly also pays to try to obtain coverage in the magazines which are read by the sort of people who may buy your product so that you are delivering your message to the broadest possible potential – as well as existing – customer base.

The professional, technical and trade magazines

Virtually all businesses have their own limited circulation publications, nearly always available on subscription only and aimed purely at the other businesses which derive their livelihood from the same kind of product as yours.

Thus, shoe manufactures – importers, distributors, wholesalers and retailers alike – may read *Shoe and Leather*

News; those involved in any way with civil engineering may read *New Civil Engineer* which is a specialist sector publication circulating only among those connected professionally with the discipline.

These publications are important to your business because a sustained level of coverage in their pages brings you firmly to the attention of trade partners, suppliers, retailers, employees, manufacturers and all those with whom you share a common interest in the heart of your business activity. They can also be used to attract investment, partnership arrangements and even mergers and takeovers without exciting comment outside trade circles or bringing you to the attention – perhaps unwelcome – of finance houses or predatory conglomerates.

Used tactically, trade media in particular can be a lifeline into some of the more respected circles of professional and trade associations and societies – the latter day guilds which can do so much to stand by a small company and help with myriad problems.

An added bonus is that such publications are usually hungry for whatever titbits of information they can find about the business; they do, after all, cater for a fairly introspective – sometimes downright incestuous – readership and items which will be of no interest whatsoever to the outside world will often receive coverage – possibly their only coverage – in the pages of this kind of publication.

Here, then, is the place to announce new appointments, new premises openings, new product lines and new promotional campaigns. This is the place where those upon whom you depend to some degree for the continuing well being of your business are bound to read about you. They are the forum in which you have the opportunity to become a figure of standing and respect in your business and professional circles.

TV and radio

These much misunderstood, much glamorized and often overhyped media have really come into their own over the last fifteen years, especially in terms of PR recognition and attention. The rise of the broadcasting industry in general has been dramatically swift and has greatly changed the course of communications in the mid-twentieth century.

Broadcasting is now the single most important medium by which to change people's opinions. Partly because of this power and partly because broadcasting is such an exciting medium, it is also an extremely wealthy business and the cost of making a mark in it is correspondingly high. Advertising rates for air time have become legendary partly because it is not a price sensitive commodity.

Even non-advertising methods of influencing the broadcasting media are expensive, not necessarily in money (although they can be) but in time, care, resources and effort. To achieve positive coverage on TV or radio is a harder task than in the printed media and it takes a dedicated effort to attain consistency of coverage, even at local level.

Stories need to have obvious visual or aural angles and often need to be broadcast on an exclusive basis. That means they must not have appeared in print before the broadcast. Producers are not averse to the story appearing subsequently in the press because it gives the public the impression that the newspapers are following the example of their programme. The power of broadcasting is such that they may well be right.

Above all, the story must come alive visually or aurally and TV producers in particular will go to great lengths to overlay programmes with a gloss of visual interest. Look, for example, at those massive BBC TV series about aspects of human development: *The Living World*, *The Ascent of Man*, *Royal Heritage* and so on. Presenters, producers, researchers, camera crews, sound crews, producers' assistants and goodness knows what else are merrily shipped off to all sorts of unlikely parts of the globe in an attempt to find a hitherto unfilmed beetle in Madagascar or an obscure fertility cult statue in Tierra del Fuego.

Above all, producers, like good journalists, are always looking for unique angles, ways in which they can present a story which will give maximum impact even if only for two minutes. Although this might not sound like a long time, it is for a TV magazine programme piece. It takes a lot of raw material to fill two minutes of airtime with worthwhile viewing or listening; hence the fragmentary nature of much broadcasting, especially at local level.

Radio, less potent than TV, has mellowed and moderated with its longer history. Cats' whiskers are no longer necessary but good, specifically targeted stories with individual angles for individual programmes most certainly are.

Local radio in particular is just as important to the PR effort as local newspapers. It doesn't just appeal to people at home; it also reaches the car driver, especially business people on their way to and from the office, the youth market and the retired. One or more of these may be the very target market for your new product.

The broadcasting media can be the difference between success and failure for your business, but do enter it cautiously and think twice before you leap; studios are littered with more failures than successes. Chapter 4 will guide you through some of the hazards.

Media people

So much for the main media channels which are, or may be, open to you. But what sort of people run these intensely competitive businesses? And what kind of people are you likely to meet if you embark upon an effort to achieve coverage in the media?

By and large, journalists themselves receive less than favourable press. They're often associated with popular images and myths. One of these is that of the weaselly investigative reporter prepared to stop at nothing to unearth the truth – however unsavoury that might be or how many people it might upset. Another is the beer swilling hack who's ambition is to get by with the minimum effort and the maximum leisure.

There is some truth in both of these characterizations – but nothing like as much as popular fiction portrays. Any profession has its share of these character types and it would be grossly out of proportion to imply that journalism suffers more than other walks of life.

Perhaps more important to the would-be PR person is the organization of the media he or she is seeking to influence. This often reflects to no little degree the personalities involved in it and a cursory glance at the way in which media operates will, as a bye-product, reveal a good deal about the kind of people who run them.

All forms of media work to extremely tight deadlines, often considerably tighter than those to which you may be accustomed. Furthermore, there is no let up in the time-tables. Your employees may consider that they work hard, and they probably do, but it's unlikely that they sustain such an effort over such a long period as a journalist.

A daily paper means just that: a full issue to create six days a week, whether there is much news around or not. There is no opportunity to take it easy the next day, for another issue is due and it must be at least as good as the previous one.

This is hard enough in itself, but the nature of creative work, such as writing, is generally in fundamental conflict with such schedules. Writing is not an art best suited to artificially imposed deadlines; it flourishes best when it is unshackled by considerations of time and space.

Moreover, the nature of the subject matter is often conducive to yet more pressure on the writer: stories which involve issues of great importance may have to be condensed into half a dozen paragraphs because there is a lot of other news around that day. This leads to savage cutting of the

original copy and accusations of shallowness and perfunc-
tory writing. But this cutting is usually carried out by subeditors and often causes as much disappointment to the
journalist who has put much hard work into the research
and writing as it does to those who make the accusations.

Furthermore, all major stories have to be checked and
double checked very rapidly and may still be sources of
disappointment, anger or, in extremis, libel action on the
part of those featured or otherwise involved.

Under such conditions, it is hardly surprising that
journalists can be a bit touchy about their role, and the
responsibility and pressure which it automatically includes.
A number of stories are potentially time-bombs; if, for
example, you are revealing the private life of a cabinet
minister or other public figure in a way which is likely to
injure his or her career, you've got to be very certain of your
facts before you go to print. If you're right, it may be
uncomfortable for them for a time; if you're wrong, you
probably need to find a new job quickly and, possibly, a
large sum of money to pay the legal damages as well.

Many journalists think of themselves as 'hacks'; most
think of each other as hacks which is always more tempting.
In fact, the term is often misused to indicate a competent
wordsmith who can write about most topics with what
appears to be an easy facility; this ease can be deceptive,
however, for no story ever really writes itself.

From a PR point of view hacks are people with as much
integrity as anyone else; they are perfectly capable of
making up their own minds about how to angle a story and
are unlikely to take kindly to blatant or clumsy efforts to
persuade them to write what somebody else would like to
see in print. Journalists' first responsibility is to their paper
and its readership – the sources of their income and security.

Do not be misled by journalists who say they can ensure
that a particular piece is included in the paper, or even one
who promises a particular slant on the write up. After

they've finished writing their story (or 'copy' as it's usually known), it is sent to the subeditors' ('subs') desk where it may be allowed through with only minor punctuation changes, where it may be emasculated or where it may be cut altogether depending on the requirements of that day's paper.

After they have submitted this copy journalists surrender control over it. The subs are also responsible for writing headlines ('House Collapse Drama; Over 1000 Bricks Injured') and subheadings to break up the appearance of the text and make the story more inviting to read.

Subs are always trained journalists who have spent some time investigating and writing articles themselves and they very often have a major input to the design and layout of a page (or 'spread') incorporating all the elements of which the journalist may be unaware such as pictures, adverts, promotions and so on.

The real day-to-day power in a newspaper, however, lies with the news editor, who has the majority of the control over what will and what won't be included in an issue. He, or she, will defer to the editor over strategic issues – such as the political complexion of the editorials – but is otherwise the manager responsible for producing the issue. He is responsible for the maintenance of editorial standards and integrity, the best balance between advertising and editorial and shares in the responsibility for sales and circulation. If you can tempt the news editor, he or she is well worth inviting to lunch.

Photographers are usually quite helpful, albeit limited in their influence. They are often freelancers, especially on local papers, which gives them – and you – access to other outlets and publications. On the basis of the old cliché that 'one picture is equal to 1000 words' they are worth cultivating.

This description of structure is greatly simplified and the bigger the paper or magazine, the more complex the lines of reporting will be. You don't need to know all about this; what you do need to remember is that the journalists you talk to may not have the discretionary power to dictate that what they write goes into the publication. In a sense, they are only the beginning of the PR process of media relations.

As a rough guideline to which kind of stories should be angled at which form of media, Figure 3 will be helpful.

Category of story	*Media type*
New/revised product	CM/L/TM
Financial story: investment, results etc.	N/L/TM
Organizational changes: plant, employees	N/L/TM
New services as extension of business	L/TM/CM
Senior appointments	N/L/TM
Other appointments	L/TM/CM
Business performance: sales, exports, orders	N/L/TM/CM
Environment/safety initiatives	N/L/TM/CM
R & D breakthroughs/research findings	N/L/TM/CM
Dealer/trade initiative	TM
Local community initiative	L/TM/CM
Charity initiative	L/TM/CM

Key: N = national media; L = local media; CM = consumer magazine; TM = trade magazine.

Figure 3 Target categories for media announcements

3   The persuasion techniques

So you've identified your story and you've identified your target media. The next stage is to put the two together by persuading journalists and broadcasters to write about your story and to do so in a responsible, positive way.

This is not a quick or easy process; it is one which requires application and persistence. It requires also a modicum of talent, especially writing ability. And it requires an element of the art of selling. Not of selling tangible products or services – this would be easy by comparison – but selling concepts, selling the idea of the story to the journalist or producer.

Selling the story can involve selling different angles to individual journalists or it can involve selling a brief resumé of the overall issue to a large number of publications. In either event, it is usually necessary to create the story in hard print so that you have a summary document to give to an interested journalist.

Clearly, this document must be well written and must also be written in such a way that the journalist has to make only minimum alterations to prepare it for publication. If the document is badly written, it may confuse him and persuade him to turn his attentions to a piece requiring less work – especially if the subject matter is of only marginal interest and he has a deadline looming.

The most common method of doing this is by the *press release*, often called the *news release*, or the *press statement*. It is a much maligned and overused device but, like democracy, it has to suffice until somebody comes up with a better way of doing things. In any case, since this is the most elementary form of press persuasion, it is a good place at which to start our look at the persuasion techniques.

The press release

The main advantage of the press release is that it enables you to reach a wide number of publications with one single piece of paper, thus ensuring consistency of message while promoting breadth of coverage. The main disadvantage is that it is such a hackneyed way of doing things that it is regarded with a world weary air by many journalists. Also, journalists receive so many press releases that they can only use a small proportion. Yours has to clamour for attention along with all the others.

Therefore, yours must be more than good, it must be *better* than most of the rest.

A survey in a leading regional newspaper a few years ago discovered that no less than 96 per cent of press releases received were consigned to the waste paper bin unused.

Among the main reasons given were:

- Lack of relevance
- The release was wrongly addressed
- Lack of newsworthiness
- The release was badly written
- The release was too overtly selling in tone.

These points deserve to be looked at one by one.

Relevance is a quality which should have been established during the stage at which you decided which publications were right for your story (see previous chapter). There is clearly very little point in sending a press release announcing a new line in pork pies to *Arab News* or circulating news of a new freight transport service to angling magazines. Your material must be relevant to the readership of the publication you choose, otherwise you're wasting its time and your own effort and money.

Targeting the right journalist on the publication has an obvious value. A release addressed to the Racing Correspondent of *Sewing Circle* is unlikely to see the light of day, no matter how exciting it might have been originally.

Try to find out about the staff on the publication you are aiming at. There are useful guides on the market which give you full details of all British and most overseas publications, details which include title, address, telephone and fax numbers, date of foundation, circulation – if known – and the names of the more prominent members of staff such as the editor, the news editor and the leading correspondents. One of the most comprehensive, and also easiest to use, is *Benn's Media Directory* which is now in its 137th edition and which contains over 650 pages of information about all sorts of outlets which afford possible PR use. It's certainly worth an investment of around £20.

Newsworthiness is perhaps the most difficult aspect for the fledgling PR person to judge. To gain admittance to the columns of a publication, a story must be worthy of note to the readership. It must have direct relevance to their interests. It must tell them something they don't already know – it must be news.

But you can't manufacture news. It may tell them something new about a familiar topic – most articles do – but it must have an original contribution to make to the overall discussion of the issue.

Here, journalists' experience counts for a great deal; because they know exactly what their readership wants. A good journalist can 'make' a relevant story out of quite unpromising material. Very few PR practitioners have access to the same intimacy with the readership and so most cannot achieve the same degree of success.

Therefore, if in doubt, try to talk through the proposed story with an experienced journalist first. He or she will know how to angle it so that it appeals to particular readerships and publications and may also advise on style, content, layout and timing.

Writing style is not something which can be acquired overnight. Indeed, creative writing of any kind is not a talent which is conspicuously widespread at all in our society and the art of 'journalese' is not easy to develop. Yet, the less work journalists have to do to the copy they receive, the more likely they are to look upon it favourably when considering how to fill space.

Perseverance can pay off. What does not pay off is sloppy writing in which clarity and meaning are unclear, technical jargon unexplained and terms are unqualified. Neither does the self-indulgence or overhyping of a story.

Selling is not something which can be overtly aimed at journalists or publications. More journalists are turned off by enthusiastic sales and marketing staff than by any other single cause. The marketing hype, the salesperson's patter, the exaggeration of your product claims, the near hysterical tone of some advertising will do more harm than good to your cause if turned on to a journalist.

Do not, therefore, be tempted to give a journalist an advert, brochure, sales leaflet, promotional kit or even a price list in isolation. Make sure that they are always used as back-up information to the release or press pack. And never let your salesperson loose on a journalist unless you, or an experienced PR operator, are there to curb his natural enthusiasm and selling style; otherwise you may find the resulting article ridicules rather than recommends.

Dunlop Slazenger
International Limited

Challenge House
Mitcham Road Croydon
Surrey CR9 3AU

Telephone 01 684 3644
Telegrams & Cables
Dunlop Slaz. Croydon.
Telex 947204 DUNSLZ

PRESS STATEMENT

Embargoed until 00.01 am 5th September 1985
THE NEW DUNLOP MAX 500GS

A revolutionary new squash racket is launched today by Dunlop Slazenger International Limited. The Dunlop MAX 500GS is unique in squash in being a hollow, injection moulded carbon fibre racket. The technology was originally devised by DSIL for the highly successful MAX 200G tennis racket used by John McEnroe.

The MAX 500GS has been developed in conjunction with Jonah Barrington who has been using it for the last nine months. Principal benefits to the player are power with extra control, less vibration, greater safety and durability.

The unique injection moulding process uses a specially blended mixture of carbon fibre and nylon. Because the frame is made in one moulding process, and because of the specially designed hollow string pillars, maximum strength is derived from the frame. Lower stringing tensions, together with the frame's inherent properties, allows players to exercise unusually accurate ball control.

Because of its unique construction, the racket absorbs more vibration than any other graphite racket, thus helping to avoid elbow and shoulder injuries in the same way as the Max 200G helps to reduce the effects of tennis elbow. DSI recommends a stringing tension of 30 lb which is lower than for wooden rackets and enhances feel and control with optimum power.

The racket's mid size head is specially designed to the maximum allowed length, but is narrower than the maximum permitted width. The result of this unique head is an ideally positioned 'sweet spot' that is elongated up the head making it easier to cope with tight shots on the walls.

Current composite rackets all have a bumper strip around the head which can break or lift with use. This wear and tear can also lead to re-stringing difficulties. The unique frame of the MAX 500GS will not splinter – an extra safety feature – and does not need a bumper strip.

Play test results suggest that the MAX 500GS is far more durable than most compression moulded rackets. Moreover, it retains the feel of a wooden racket but combines this with the power of compression graphite.

Commenting on the racket Jonah Barrington said, 'I have never before played with a racket with such a unique combination of lightness and power, control and vibration dampening. The optimum head size and the ideally positioned 'sweet spot' make control easier, no matter how much power you put behind the shot. I think it has helped me to develop my game even further and its impact on the market is going to be terrific.'

For further information please contact:

A R Greener
Director of Communications & Publicity
Dunlop Slazenger International Limited
Challenge House
Mitcham Road
CROYDON CR9 3AU   Telephone 01-684-3644

OR

G Baird
Squash Product Manager
Dunlop Slazenger International Limited
Challenge House
Mitcham Road
CROYDON
CR9 3AU   Telephone 01-684-3644

Figure 4   Dunlop Slazenger International Ltd press release for MAX500GS in 1985

Some golden rules

So, having looked at what *not* to do when creating and targeting your press release, what do you *do*? There are a few golden rules – and a great deal of commonsense – which will help to give your releases at least a sporting chance of seeing the light of day again after they leave your office.

First, be brief. Try to condense your whole story into no more than eight paragraphs, fewer if possible. Be ruthless in cutting out any unnecessary information and all redundant words and phrases. You will be amazed at how succinctly you can then express yourself.

Second, ensure that the gist of the story is contained in the first paragraph, preferably in the first sentence. There should be no more than two sentences in the first paragraph in any case, and these should summarize the rest of the document so that a journalist need look no further to decide whether to use it or not. (He or she probably won't read more than the first paragraph anyway; you don't get a second chance.)

Third, keep the English as simple and everyday as possible. Remember the *Sun*. The readers you are aiming at might prefer that kind of direct approach because it is clearer and more understandable. Avoid using long words for the sake of it. Where you're dealing with complex issues, try to introduce a simple example demonstrating what you mean. Be prepared to simplify your terminology (the journalist will, so you might as well get used to it).

Try to avoid technical jargon with specialized meanings and obscure terms. If the nature and subject matter of the story dictate that you must use technical jargon, then make sure it's explained in simple, clear layman's language. Call a spade a spade, not a manual earth moving implement. And avoid pretension. Maximize your achievements or products by all means, but don't claim that they are what they are not.

Fourth, pay attention to your layout. There is a generally accepted form of laying out a press release which at least shows the journalist that you know what you're doing.

Always give the release a heading and a date at the top. Always set out the document in space-and-a-half or double spacing. A closely printed document is harder to read, harder to annotate and harder to edit. Leave plenty of room in broad margins for scribbled annotations.

Make sure that your name, address and telephone number are clearly set out at the bottom as a source of further information. (And make sure that there's somebody competent sitting at the end of the phone to handle the calls – preferably, you.)

Fifth, use quotes where they add to the credibility, but use them sparingly and never at the beginning of the piece. They can be added at the end so that the journalist can include them if there is space. Coming higher up, they smack of self-aggrandizement and are likely to cause the whole release to be binned. If possible, use a third party to endorse your product, service or statement and one who is well enough known as an authority to carry some weight.

Sixth, don't expect a piece of paper to solve all your publicity requirements. Follow it up with a phone call if you can, sell a feature or two around it, include or offer a photograph if appropriate, invite a journalist to a follow-up meeting or interview – anything to capitalize on the attention your release may have gained. The release is a device to bring you and your business to the attention of the media and a *basic* statement of your story – no more.

How do these 'rules' apply to a real life example? And what further details might add to the credibility and professionalism of your release?

The press release announcing the new Dunlop MAX500GS squash racket shown in Figure 4 dates from 1985 and was produced in response to a number of requirements:

1 It had to launch a new flagship product.
2 It had to announce a new application of technology unique to Dunlop.
3 It had to reflect the huge success achieved by the same technology in tennis, in the shape of the MAX200G tennis racket, and also refer to its prime user at that time, John McEnroe.
4 It had to maximize the company's investment in retaining the services of Jonah Barrington, Britain's best-known and most successful squash player.
5 It had to appeal to both specialist squash media as well as more generalized national and regional newspapers and magazines.

6 It had to explain the benefits of the technology in language which anyone interested in squash – or tennis – could understand without leaping for a dictionary.

Given this background, how does it measure up against our 'golden rules'?

First of all, it's short: eight paragraphs to cover a fairly technical subject.

Second, the whole story is contained in the first two sentences. The two sentences in the first paragraph rule is deliberately broken here in order to allow mention of a proven headline grabber (John McEnroe) in the first paragraph as well. This had the effect of interesting non-squash journalists to read further.

Third, the language is as simple as possible for a technological story. It does not talk down to the reader, yet it describes the detail quite simply.

Fourth, the layout follows the classic formula and includes an embargo date and time. This was necessary because the release was designed to be used in conjunction with three regional media and dealer launches in the UK, all of which took place on different days. Therefore, the whole story had to be held back until this tour was completed as its first appearance in print would have rendered the remaining events useless. Once written up in the media in one part of the UK, a product story is deemed to have been launched throughout the country and ceases to be news.

Fifth, it uses Jonah Barrington in an approved quote, thus adding the weight of a positive product endorsement from a greatly respected and universally recognized authority.

Sixth, it clearly sets out the contact points for further information.

Preparing the way and following up
The press release in itself is not enough to turn a low profile topic into a high profile public debate. Indeed, you may

write a number of perfectly good, workmanlike releases and never see one of them in print unless you:

1 prepare the way first, and
2 follow up the release with a phone call.

What both of these actions do is to *establish contact* with the media – the most important part of any media relations programme. It is essential that the recipients of your stories know a bit about the outfit from whom they are receiving them, otherwise they will find it impossible to place them in context and will probably ignore them in favour of something easier or more familiar.

You need a good excuse to make contact with a writer you've never met, who's never heard of you and who has many other interests. A follow-up to a strong release is a good way; it's then that you can turn on the full service by:

1 Introducing yourself.
2 Asking whether he or she received the release. (If not, get another one posted or, preferably biked, round as quickly as possible.)
3 Asking whether it was of interest.
4 Asking whether they would like clarification or amplification on any points.
5 Asking whether they have enough good photographs.
6 Asking whether he or she would like to meet the person responsible for the initiative in the story with a view to writing a rather more in-depth feature than could be based on a press release.
7 Inviting them to see or test the product for themselves or see the factory in which it's made.

All these are simply excuses to grab the time and attention of the journalist and direct him or her towards the fuller writing up of your story. Sometimes you hit lucky and come across one or more writers who are genuinely very interested in your story. The Dunlop squash racket wasn't a difficult topic to sell, partly because of the popularity of the sport among journalists and partly because it was linked to a chance to meet Jonah Barrington, almost a legend in the game and something of a recluse in his Glastonbury fastness.

The benefits – and the objectives – of this contact are far more lasting than one story. If created properly, they establish a relationship of mutual business value; you have information which the journalist needs or wants from time to time and he has access to the means of publicizing that information for the benefit of your enterprise.

In order to write authoritatively about your business however, the journalist needs to know something about its background: what the total market is and what the emerging trends might be, perhaps, and how your product or service is aimed at a particular niche in that market; who the really important people are (or the more reticent ones) and what's happening generally in the industry.

Thus, the state of British and world squash was a natural topic for journalists who received the Dunlop announcement. So was the current position of Jonah's career (usually a matter of some speculation by interested journalists), the changes in technology that were then revolutionizing rackets and other squash equipment, the promising young players (especially those sponsored by Dunlop), the chances of the established players (and particularly whether anyone could beat Jehangir Khan), everything, in fact, which comprised the politics, general background and even gossip of the sport.

Journalists can learn some of this information from their own sources, but are unlikely to be able to obtain full or official confirmation without access to specialists.

The mutual benefits
Sometimes, you will have to do a bit of horse trading.

Remember that the journalist is always on the look out for a good story.

If in the course of your normal activities you happen to come across information which, without betraying confidences, approaches the nature of a juicy titbit, then it may be no skin off your nose to share it with someone who appreciates it more than you do.

But, be very careful. Information given in innocence can be twisted out of all recognition, especially by an irresponsible reporter out to make a quick name for himself. You have to know exactly what you're doing and, even more importantly, what he's doing, before you can safely risk giving away information which is not normally available.

If you can achieve this without hurting anyone, however, you'll probably find it a useful way of:

1 Receiving favourable attention from that journalist when you've got a less than gripping story for which you want coverage, and
2 Keeping in touch with what's happening elsewhere in your field of activity.

Treated cautiously and cleverly, it can act as a private information gathering system. Bungled, it can land both you and the journalist in a great deal of hot water....

I once knew a company, for example, where it often used to be recognized practice to leak the contents of a letter to employees to the local media, sometimes before the letter itself was sent out, especially before or during an industrial dispute. This had the effect of publicizing the management's viewpoint far more widely than could otherwise have been the case and, what was even more important, it delivered the message straight to the employees' homes and families in a way that appeared to be an impartial, third party recording of events and attitudes.

It was all strictly unofficial, although everyone knew that it was being done, and, for a while, it greatly assisted in strengthening the company's relationship with the local media. After a while, they tumbled to the ruse and realized that they were being used as an extension of the company propaganda machine but, by that time, media relationships were more harmonious and no lasting harm was done.

This sort of information is usually termed 'off the record', the implication being that the journalist will either not use it at all or, if he or she does, will never reveal its source. Although loyalty rates are high, the only safe way of approaching this normally is to assume that everything is *on* the record. The relationship with the journalist is unlikely to suffer and, if you do receive less than glowing reports in the publication concerned, perhaps it just means that you need to find more meaty stories.

Another useful way of cultivating media awareness is to let it be known that you have experts or authorities on a number of topics who are prepared to give an opinion on a subject which might come up in the course of daily news coverage. Thus, when working at one of the Midlands universities a stone's throw from the two local TV stations, I supplied them both with a list of academics who were prepared to comment upon aspects of the news. In this way, a number of academics gained useful experience in broadcasting and several went on to command considerable respect and attention from TV over the next few years.

One economics professor, for example, was asked to go into the studios to comment on the Budget as the Chancellor was making his speech – something many of us would, no doubt, like to do.

Without aspiring to this level, you can often command coverage for yourself and your business by simply being willing to help a journalist when needed. Such attitudes and assistance are remembered and, usually, acknowledged in some form at some time.

The visit

Invitations to visit factories or other centres of activity are often appreciated because journalists (who need to know a little about a very wide variety of topics) are often grateful for help in reducing the learning curve they inevitably experience.

There are a few rules here which will help to derive the best from the day.

1 Make sure the place – and the workforce – are as clean as can be reasonably expected. Dirty and untidy premises denote a lack of pride on the part of those who own, manage and operate them.

2 Make sure that, without obviously planting tame 'Company men', you don't give the local militant a free hit at your employee relations policies. Likewise, make sure that you observe the courtesies of informing the unions and all those through whose areas the visitor will pass. Nothing is more annoying to employees than to have to watch a string of unknown visitors parade past as though they were visiting the zoo. This is exacerbated if the employees have not been told who the visitors are, let alone why they're visiting.

3 Don't let a journalist leave without some token of hospitality. Four course lunches are neither necessary nor desirable, but a buffet lunch, or, at least a drink and a snack of some sort, are essential.

4 Don't let the journalist leave either without a written record of the major points of what's been seen, even if this may have to be produced specially for the occasion. It will always come in handy for the next time and the chances of the journalist retaining the key information is greatly increased. (Full press packs are essential for larger scale visits.)

5 Don't try to 'over-produce' the visit. Don't force the guest to talk to anyone if he or she doesn't want to or force

an unwilling employee to give an interview. Don't put on a sales pitch, although a product demonstration is often appreciated. And don't submerge your guest in an avalanche of irrelevant or marketing-based information; it probably won't be read and it certainly won't be appreciated.

Above all, the visit shows a willingness to be open with a journalist; an honest approach which he or she will find reassuring when dealing with your subsequent media coverage requests. It demonstrates that, not only do you have nothing to hide, but that you are quite prepared to let them see that fact for themselves. Consequently it puts your future relationship on a footing of mutual trust: the first essential in any dealing with the media.

The event
The visit in itself is an event, albeit a low key one. There is, however, a more ambitious category known as the 'Press Event' for which rather more elaborate preparations are necessary.

It may take the form of a new product launch, a product test day, a specialist conference involving third parties, a demonstration of a particular aspect of your work, or it may be simply an excuse for a binge – something which is hardly unknown in the PR world.

This is an altogether more formal occasion and one which will require more organization and effort than the un-official, one-off visit; consequently, the subject is treated fully in Chapter 5.

The device
The 'device' is an event or action which is undertaken not so much for itself as for its ability to create media coverage opportunities, for example, publicity stunts and other

promotional events. In this context the device is an extension of the legitimate event or promotion and the dividing line can sometimes be difficult to discern.

One of the easiest ways to buy coverage is the '*advertorial*', a simple but effective device to gain media space without it looking obvious that you've bought it. In practice, it is a deal negotiated with a publication whereby you pay for a certain amount of space (say, one page) and are given another, equal, amount free for the insertion of an article which complements the advert. Sometimes you write your own article; sometimes the publication will do it for you and submit it for your approval.

A variation on both advertising and editorial and an uneasy halfway house between the two, the advertorial is usually resorted to at times when the available material will not command editorial mention in its own right or when the detailed wording of an article is of the utmost importance.

If you're desperate for coverage and can't get it any other way, it's a useful method.

The competition
This is another well tried and tested device, the main purpose of which is to achieve coverage without having a strong enough story. It can be organized either through a publication ('Spot the Ball and Win a Sunshine Fiesta') or it can be run as a product-based exercise, with entry forms in the product packaging. In this case coverage is secondary to increased sales ('Identify seven knobbly knees – complete the tie breaker (using your skill and judgement of course) – and send in your entry along with 26,000 sticky wrappers.')

Competitions run through a publication have the obvious advantage that you are virtually guaranteed coverage in its pages. Conversely, the disadvantage is that no other publication in its right mind will touch the story because it promotes another publication as well as your product.

Some national papers are now insisting on a minimum prize value that may make you think twice before ringing the Promotions Desk of the *Daily Blank*. £1,000 is becoming the accepted norm and, in practice, the true value of the prize can be considerably higher, especially when you consider the extra marketing effort which is needed to take full advantage of the results.

The competition is not without other perils. As mentioned earlier, I was once called in by an eminent company which was very concerned that the results of a nationwide competition had been deliberately rigged in order to provide a wide geographic spread of winners, thereby improving the coverage in the local media. Fortunately, the accusation turned out to be a combination of fiction and circumstantial evidence but, even so, it cost the company a very large sum of money and not a few sleepless nights in the process of keeping any scandal away from the gutter press.

The moral is, therefore, to be sure that you're purer than pure, and can prove that everyone who has ever had anything to do with the idea is in a similar state of grace.

Charity promotions

These promotions always strike both me and a number of my colleagues as slightly suspect. Maybe it's because there's always a suspicion that ostentatious altruism is an inevitable contradiction in terms. Whatever the reason, whether it's justified or not, this is an area of which a good many PR operators steer clear.

If you must do it, choose your charity carefully. Go for a non-political, well-established and highly respectable cause, preferably one which has a medical benefit such as Cancer Research or the British Heart Foundation. Don't get sidetracked into supporting a local, amateurish and unheard of cause. It might be perfectly respectable and deserving of your money, in which case give it a cheque and enter the amount in your books so that your accountant can derive the maximum tax benefits.

On the other hand, it might be a fly-by-night front for the laundering of ill-gotten gains and, although ignorance might save you from legal difficulties, you're still going to have egg all over your face if the case comes to court and the reporting restrictions are lifted.

Awards

Pot hunting isn't confined to sporting occasions. The country is swarming with organizations that will give awards for something or other, most of them highly respectable establishments whose accolades automatically command column inches.

The Queen's Awards to Industry, for example, are very useful for publicity purposes and remarkably attainable in a painless sort of way. There are two categories – Services to Technology and Services to Exports – and the only real rule is that you can't win both kinds in the same year. You're allowed to display the Royal Crest on all aspects of your business for a period of five years following the award and the media coverage can be reward enough in itself. The awards are granted and announced annually and further information is available from the Queen's Award Office on 01 212 5271.

Another good old warhorse for PR exploitation is the Design Council Award scheme. This is also annual and involves a sort of prize-giving at which a winning company has the opportunity to blow its own trumpet to a remarkable degree. Again, a coveted logo is part of the prize and British industry takes this one very seriously.

The basis on which prizes are awarded is rather more subjective (or mysterious) than the Queen's Awards. The four-door Range Rover achieved one in 1982 largely for the addition – long overdue – of two more doors to a body shell designed in the late 1960s. (Further details from the Design Council on 01 839 8000.)

Sponsorship

This is such a minefield of traps and opportunities that it is dealt with in Chapter 7. Sponsorship can be a very effective method of focusing attention on your business; it can also be a rapid method of pouring money down the drain.

As a general rule, for modest PR requirements, stick to sponsoring something small and local like a carnival float or a fence in the village gymkhana. In this way your exposure will be limited, although you reach your local target audience, but the extent of your liability will also be very manageable.

Professional sport and, to a lesser extent, the arts are big business and you need a correspondingly big cheque book and a stoical approach to the fate of its contents if you are to participate in sponsorship at this level.

The observance of one simple rule, however, can provide a reasonable insurance policy: provide sponsorship in kind, not in cash. Supply your product or service on a limited basis either free or at a rate which covers your costs. You will still receive all the usual acknowledgements in programmes and on posters, but you will be protected from the liability of putting considerable sums of money at risk.

The gimmick

Devices that focus attention on your business are all very well, providing support for a needy or worthy cause and providing you with a modest amount of publicity for a modest outlay into the bargain. There is, however, an extension of this principle which is not quite so watertight: the adoption of a gimmick to grab media coverage.

Gimmicks can take all sorts of forms – usually publicity stunts involving relatively zany activities reminiscent of the Hollywood antics of the 1920s and 1930s, such as standing on the wings of an acrobatic aircraft or jolly japes from student days, such as trying to cross the Thames in a bathtub.

There is usually a market for this kind of bizarre story, especially among the pop tabloids, but it is gradually fading and seldom extends to the more serious papers in which you may feel that your business will receive more dignified, and relevant, coverage.

There are many more gimmicks than we have space to list: hot air balloon races, giant entry cards or tickets, half naked ladies draped across the product (formerly the favourite Motor Show gimmick), and other vapid products of febrile imaginations. They sometimes achieve their objectives, but usually only when they are so original that they constitute a first. Follow-up exercises or imitation acts can make journalists grow tired of the same, basically irrelevant, formula and look elsewhere for a story.

The value of the gimmick, therefore, lies in its originality. Too many pale imitations negate the original idea and spoil the chances of any future coverage. So, if you must indulge in gimmickry, come up with the one-off, an idea that will achieve its objective of a few photos in the papers and can then be decently laid to rest.

As an example, the Festival of Thailand in 1987 was a notoriously difficult event to publicize in advance, partly because very few of the exhibits were in the UK more than a few days before the Festival opened. One exhibit that was available however was a tuk-tuk. This is a little, three-wheeled motor cycle taxi that potters about the streets of Bangkok. An invitation to *Motor* magazine to road test this vehicle like an ordinary car met with an enthusiastic response and a very favourable feature article, partly because tuk-tuks would never otherwise be seen in the Western world.

The placed interview

This is the best method of achieving an in-depth account of an important aspect of your business and is likely to reflect quite closely the emphasis that you wish to put upon the topic. It is also harder to achieve than many other kinds of media coverage because it occupies more editorial space than the write up of, say, a press release. Also, readers want to read about an intrinsically interesting subject if they are to embark upon a feature article – and your business might not be quite interesting enough to command that kind of attention span.

It is a fact that the average reading age of the UK is fourteen. That is to say, the majority of the population do not wish to (and may not be capable of) reading material more complicated than a relatively advanced book by Enid Blyton. Consequently, newspapers and magazines always need articles written to appeal to elementary reading ability. This often means that they must be short, simple and to the point – all the qualities which are difficult to achieve in an interview-based feature.

Moreover, interviews seldom contain hard news. There may be a news feature, but this is usually reserved for issues of rather more national importance than the health of your business – unless you happen to be the Chief Executive of BA or British Coal.

There are, therefore, two main points to bear in mind concerning placed interviews. The first is to target the publication very carefully; the second is to ensure that you, or the interviewee, are going to say something original and relatively weighty.

If, for example, you own or run a company which manufactures and sells billiard balls, you may find it difficult to persuade the *Times* to allocate half a page for an interview with you on the strength of respectable sales figures but a worrying downturn in the order book.

You'd be much better off talking to one of the trade publications which reaches the retailers who sell – or who could sell – your products for you, such as *Sports Retailing* or *Harpers Sports and Leisure*. In their pages you are relevant to the readership and what you have to say will be of some interest to them as well as carrying a highly relevant publicity benefit to you.

Your chances will be strengthened greatly if you can offer as the angle to the interview a discussion on a broader aspect of the business which might strike an answering chord among the readers. This might be something pertinent to the billiard industry and retailing fraternity – such as the danger posed by cheap, Far Eastern imports, or the difficulties facing the sport following a major reduction in TV coverage. Then you have a topic which is of more general interest and you still achieve your objective of publicizing your company and its strengths by working in examples of your business and ensuring that your brand name is mentioned a few times, especially in the introduction. (Don't overdo the brand mentions; relentless name dropping will turn off both publication and reader alike.)

Interview features, then, tend to address the 'state of the nation' topics: the trends facing a particular industry as exemplified by your business experience.

This may also call you to the attention of trade associations and other professional bodies so that you find that you receive invitations to speak at trade conferences and similar events. This in itself can do both you and your company a great deal of good. You become known as an authority on your subject, especially within your industry; therefore, your product is likely to be both a familiar name and a good buy. In the eyes of many consumers, familiarity equals reassurance. You then enter the spiral of success based on higher sales, leading to increased knowledge of your brand, while greater knowledge of your brand reassures consumers that they are buying from a market leader and this, in turn, creates higher sales. At this stage you can order the Mercedes coupé.

Feature articles

Feature articles do not have to be based on interviews, although it is likely that interviews will be required at some stage in order to lend credibility and authority to the assertions contained in the features. There are other ways of achieving an in-depth survey in a publication.

One is to write the article yourself and 'sell it in' to the editor. This requires a fair amount of writing skill and a great deal of selling skill. It also requires you to have a fresh outlook on what may be a fairly tired, overwritten topic. You must have something new to contribute and it must be expressed in a way which is interesting and easily understood.

A safer method of obtaining a feature is to interest a journalist in the subject you want publicized and let him or her write it for you. It's then far more likely to be accepted by the editor and you still have the opportunity to control what is said to some degree.

It is as necessary to invent an angle upon which the feature can be hung as it is important to be offering a genuine news story in a press release.

You might, for example, consider the publication of all, or part, of the findings of research which you have either conducted yourself or commissioned. If the latter, make sure that you have the copyright before letting a journalist loose on the findings. (Obtaining the copyright is usually a simple matter of paying the invoice in full, but there can be unseen traps which are usually hidden in the small print.)

Human interest features are another angle for a paper, especially those with heart warming stories of children or animals achieving something against all odds. Editors often like to be seen to be bringing stories of courage and heroism to the fore as an illustration of the good that their publications can do in helping people to overcome difficulties. Bob Champion's successful fight against cancer and subsequent winning of the Grand National was a splendid example. Make sure that you don't allow the piece to become mawkish however. That will turn off all the readers.

Stories about your employees are very good for internal relations purposes as well as for external use. Someone who jumps into a river to save a dog from drowning or wins the football pools is almost guaranteed to make at least the local paper and maybe some of the nationals as well if sold in hard enough and if not faced with major competition from other news.

No matter what angle you can create, remember you are not paying for advertising, and you cannot tell the journalist what to write, nor can you complain if your company or brand name is not included as often as you would like. If the story has been distorted to your detriment you can, of course, complain and should do. At worst you'll probably receive an apology and at best a follow-up piece putting the record straight and giving further exposure to your company.

Above all, features must contain enough meat to keep a readership happy for about five minutes reading. Magazine features are good examples to study. The December 1988 issue of *Options for Men* including 'Keith Richard, the Rolling Stone going it alone', 'The driving forces behind the Car of the Year', 'A day in the diary of James Oliver' (the man who is set to become the 1990s answer to Carl Jung), 'The Wright to Reply' (the man who beat the British spy system), and 'Let the Rot set in' (hedonists look out, the future is bleak). None of these were particularly good feature articles as it happens, but they do show the broad range of topics which attract up to 2500 words and for which people will pay money.

The photo

The old PR cliché is that a picture is worth a thousand words, recognizing that the human brain accepts visual material more readily than the written word; hence the massive growth of TV, cinema and video – the visual media which tell stories by using moving pictures.

Indeed, consider a video instead of – or as well as – a piece of paper for an annual report, for example, or a message to the workforce or a 'video release'. It's more expensive, but it's also far more effective.

The static visual (the photograph) remains good value however and will certainly gain attention in most publications. There are two ways of going about getting a picture published: either take the picture yourself (or have it taken) and submit it to the picture desk, or interest the paper in the subject and persuade them to send a photographer to cover the occasion.

As with the feature article, it's well worth trying to get the publication to do the work for you. Not only will their photographers know the style the paper requires and how the editor's mind works, they will also often have useful suggestions on how the story can be made more visual and dramatic.

Also, most publications often use freelance photographers. They can be of great value in recommending other outlets for the pictures they take of your subject matter. They are paid by everyone who uses their work so it is in their interest to sell as many of their photos as possible.

Above all, the professional will be able to inject into the photos all the right elements of impact, drama, movement and clarity that the publication needs. However good a photographer you may be, you do not necessarily know the requirements of the newspaper's picture desk.

Some photography is still shot in black and white although the development of more sophisticated printing techniques at affordable prices means that a great many more publications are now making a sales point of colour pages. Nevertheless, the day has not yet come when black and white 5 × 8s have been ousted and this is the format which should accompany your releases. A note sent with them offering colour transparencies often leads to colour being used instead.

Captions to photos

Captions are very important. Without them, the picture will almost certainly not be used. Likewise, if the photographer from the paper is taking the shots he, or she, will certainly need to know exactly what he's shooting before he takes his film back to the paper.

If you're writing the captions yourself, they should be clear, short and simple, telling the outlines of the story in not more then two sentences – one if you can manage it. Occasionally, a paper will request a 'deep' caption. This usually means that you can go to half a dozen lines. If so, be careful not to repeat yourself. Describe what's happening in the picture and why, but not the whole context of the incident or the editor will cut out the whole piece.

Captions have an uncanny knack of becoming separated from photographs in a newspaper office so always include your name and phone number on both.

If you are around when the pictures are being taken, don't try to overproduce the results. Photographers don't appreciate being told what to shoot any more than journalists appreciate being told what to write. They're both free thinkers and they both need to be told the bare essentials. Anything else they need to know, they'll ask you.

So don't try to get your logo in the background on every picture; the fact that you're getting into the paper at all should be reward enough. And don't try to dictate where or when it should be shot. Photographers know what they want. That's not to say that they might not be grateful for a few suggestions here and there, but don't go beyond that and don't try to overinfluence the end result. If the photographer wants a producer, he can always send for Cecil B de Mille.

In conclusion

Persuading writers, photographers, editors and producers to feature your story is a complex art and one which can only ever be really successful with experience of the media concerned. But the observation of these very basic ground rules will do two things:

First, it will show your media contacts that you have some knowledge of the circumstances in which they work. This is important because most people do not have this insight. (Try to visit a newspaper office or a TV studio sometime; its a fascinating and eye-opening experience.)

Second, it will demonstrate a willingness to be co-operative to the media and that is an investment essential to the success of your PR career.

It is surprising how many attempts are made to influence the media without any regard whatsoever for these ground rules; consequently, the media runs what it is forced to run in the absence of any enlightenment or co-operation. The usual consequence of this is that the media is dubbed irresponsible or biased; yet, the old law of the jungle applies in full: know your enemy and he becomes much less formidable.

4 TV and radio

TV and radio are different from the written press; consequently, they require different rules and different approaches.

Both media are, for a start, instantaneous in a way that the printed word cannot yet be. News is literally news on either TV or radio – a story which has just broken and which has probably not yet been picked up by any newspaper. Even if it has, the paper's next edition is unlikely to be on sale until the next day by which time the broadcast media will have wrung every last shred of originality out of it.

Both BBC television and ITV have three major news bulletins a day – at lunchtime, early evening and mid/late evening. These are roughly aimed respectively at the housewife and retired audience, the family and early work leavers and business people and later work leavers. It follows, therefore, that each bulletin has a different emphasis and that a story which made the lunchtime news might not be included later.

Radio can be even more instantaneous. There are news bulletins usually every hour on major channels and local stations throughout the day with hardly less frequent readings during the night.

Radio is not just for senior citizens who love the *Archers* or yearn for a return of *Mrs Dale's Diary*. It is one of the best ways of reaching an audience quaintly known as the 'driving-to-work' or the 'driving-home' audience. In other words, it reaches the car driver and particularly, the commuter – especially outside the South-East where rail commuting is less necessary.

It reaches, therefore, a large number of business people as they sit in cars between, roughly, 7 and 9 in the morning and 4.30 and 7 in the evening. And, even if the listener's not stuck in a traffic jam, the chances are he or she wants to hear the news on two levels; national and local.

Moreover, research suggests that the higher number of tape players in cars over the last ten years has done little or nothing to discourage the commuter from listening to the radio, at least for the news bulletins. With the increased popularity of car phones, many drivers are now joining phone-in programmes as well. Ironically, new automotive gadgetry has helped give the relatively old-fashioned radio a new lease of life.

The recognized pulling power of TV is almost legendary. Thousands of millions of pounds are spent each year on TV advertising, much of it at astronomical rates because TV is the single most powerful persuader in our society. As such, it behoves any aspiring PR function to achieve at least some coverage, somewhere.

Getting into broadcasting

So, what can you do about getting into broadcasting? Which TV and radio programmes could take your stories? How do you go about selecting them? And, once selected, how do you go about selling in your material?

Unsurprisingly, the answers are a little more complex than those to the same questions about the press. Any broadcast medium is a complex business and, in order to stand much of a chance of having your stories accepted, you need to know a little about the way in which TV and radio stations are run.

Fundamentally, your story must have a number of qualities in much the same way as the stories for newspapers or periodicals. It must be a genuine story, announcing something that nobody knew before and in which the watching or listening public has an interest.

Second, with very few exceptions, it must not have been written about previously in the media to any significant extent. If it appeared in yesterday's evening paper or this morning's daily, then you're wasting your time attempting to persuade TV or radio to take it. What's more, you're likely to insult the professionalism of the producers concerned if you even try, and that won't stand you in good stead for the next time you want coverage. In other words, it must be a *true* exclusive.

The main exception to this rule is the learned or professional journal which is not on sale to the general public. If, for instance, you have invented a new fire extinguisher and it has so far been seen only in the *Fireman's Gazette* (if there was such a publication) then TV and radio are still options and should not be ruled out. But, by and large, exclusivity is a prerequisite to broadcast coverage.

I once persuaded the BBC television programme *Pebble Mill at One* to run a piece on a motorway accident kit invented by one of the academics at Aston University. The introductory discussions went well, the kit lived up to its revolutionary approach and actually worked when it was supposed to – not always a foregone conclusion with any invention. The academic, or 'boffin' as the TV people insisted on calling him, rehearsed reasonably well when faced with a real live interviewer and all looked set fair for the inclusion of the piece which was being broadcast live.

We were having a last bracer in the bar before going on when the academic casually threw away the remark that this particular invention hadn't worked too well the last time it was on TV but it was much more reliable now. The silence in the bar was awful. The director asked, very quietly and ominously, for clarification. So did I, for it was the first I knew about it.

It transpired that a regional magazine programme somewhere in Scotland had featured the kit about three years previously – not something which you would think would have been particularly relevant. The director quietly gave orders for the item to be replaced by a standby piece already shot on film. Then he turned to me and said 'What does it feel like to be the ex-Information Officer for the University of Aston?' We then turned our attention to the bar in real earnest.

The relationship survived and the programme and the University continued to co-operate, but, as somebody or other said about the Battle of Waterloo, it was a close run thing.

The third cardinal point is relevance. Relevance to the programme's central theme or the region covered by the station, or a topic which is on everybody's lips that day. It doesn't matter which, provided the story sits naturally in the programme and doesn't look contrived.

A new factory offering new jobs, for instance, is a good example of a story which is relevant to the local TV and radio stations. A new application of technology which affects people's lives – preferably for the better – is a good example of the kind of story that might go on *Tomorrow's World*. A good samaritan rescue act which enables a group of relatively deprived individuals to achieve something that would otherwise be impossible for them is potentially good material for a socially conscious programme, whether local or national.

But, be careful. New products are, in themselves, not deemed suitable fodder for the impartial and non-commercial broadcasting media. If they have a particular slant which is relevant, like creating new jobs, easing the plight of the underprivileged or achieving the equivalent of taking coals to Newcastle, then that could be a different matter. But you are going to have to be very sensitive and subtle in the way in which you go about selling the idea.

All broadcast media are very sensitive about the role of broadcasting in the UK. They take very differing lines on its exact role in the community but on one point they are almost unanimous: broadcasting does not exist to serve the commercial sector. In this, you may think that they ignore the vast revenues which are pumped into broadcasting by various commercial enterprises – but this in no way makes any easier the task of having material accepted.

One point which sounds self-evident, but which often catches out the unwary, is that the whole essence of TV is built around a visual platform. Images succeed one another on the screen, building up an impression that the producer wants to convey. Yet, many PR outfits fail to realize this most elementary of rules and bombard unfortunate producers with material which is anything but visual – static, dull, complicated or boring; sometimes all at the same time.

By the same token, radio is aural; if a story cannot be captured in the spoken word, then it's no good trying to place it on the radio, no matter how strong it might be otherwise. One surprisingly common faux pas is the PR practitioner who sends a press release to a radio station with the accompanying photographs.

Essentially the story must suit the medium at which you are aiming it. If it is not, and cannot be made, visual, then TV is a waste of time; far better to wait until you have a really good story and get them to do it properly.

Almost invariably a press release is also a waste of time. Few TV or radio reporters like to think of themselves as hacks and few will deign to use the words of even the best PR writer without a thorough re-write. In fairness, this is sometimes necessary anyway, but there is another element at work here: the element of broadcasting superiority.

One of the rewards – and penalties – of coming into contact with literally millions of people through broadcasting is the consequent fame and recognition. Simply reading the news (not a terribly demanding job) can bring untold rewards in terms of public recognition, appearances and wealth. Top news readers' salaries are a nonsense and bear no relationship to their ability. What they do reflect, is the pulling power – almost the entertainment rating – of the news reader. Whether that is right or wrong need not concern us; what is important is the understanding that broadcasting is one of the worst places for inflated egos.

Being constantly in front of a microphone or camera can turn the sanest of individuals into veritable showmen or women. Any attempt to sell in a story must reflect this self-regard. So, do not simply bung them a press release and expect to see it regurgitated on the screen or read out on the sound waves. Far more subtle methods are required.

Selling the story

Let's assume you have a reasonable story with most of the attractive ingredients. You are opening a new processing plant in an area where it will create a significant number of new jobs – always a good, emotive topic – and will also contribute to the balance of trade by exporting 80 per cent of its output to Japan. Just to gild the lily, there has been a significant investment in robotics and other automated processes, something which always makes good, visual television. A good scenario, but how do you get it on to the silver screen?

The first step, as with a conventional press release, is to target the programme. In this case, the local news magazine programme will almost certainly be interested if it's put to them in the right way. This is the regional 'opt out' which runs in the early evening for about half an hour in most parts of, the country, usually between 6 and 7. If the story is good enough, they will probably attempt to sell it in to the national news programmes themselves – and they have a far greater chance of success than you are ever likely to achieve.

If your telephone voice and manner are good, try ringing the editor or producer yourself. The names will be listed in the *Radio Times* or *TV Times*. The chances are that you will get fobbed off by the switchboard and put through to the News Desk. That's OK; they'll be the ones who'll have to create the story, if it happens, in any case.

Whoever you talk to, keep it brief and relevant. Have a short note in front of you of the merits of the story for that particular programme - in this case, 'Regional investment, new jobs, advanced robotics and high export content.'

Ten words like that can do more to sell a story to the broadcasting media than a whole screed of salesman's blurb. If he or she is interested, they'll take it further – once they've established that they are getting a 'first', nobody else has run the story before them and is unlikely to do so.

If you don't trust yourself to achieve this on the phone, then write the producer or editor a letter, setting out the same message and stressing your willingness to let the programme have exclusivity. Keep it short, never more than one page and only one sentence on each of the major selling points. Second pages aren't read in the broadcasting world.

If both of these approaches fail, try the other TV channel. If this fails, re-assess your story.

Roughly similar methods work with radio producers and editors; the major difference is that they tend to be less arrogant about having exclusives and are often more approachable. In any case, radio has more magazine type airtime to fill, there are far more accessible radio programmes than TV programmes and the chances of hitting it off with at least one are therefore rather higher.

Preparing for the filming

If you gain the attention of the editor, the next stage is to prepare for the arrival of a producer, sometimes alone, sometimes accompanied by a film crew.

This visit is the 'Recce' in which they will decide what they will film, and when, how and who they will talk to. The art here is to try to influence decisions as much as possible without jeopardizing the piece going ahead. (The presence of a producer does not necessarily mean that the piece will be filmed; he can always recommend to the editor that the story is not strong enough and that will probably be the end of your coverage.)

So it is worth taking the time and trouble to be more than helpful; make sure the producer sees everything that he or she wants. There's no point in trying to hide things from a person who's going to introduce your new factory – and therefore your company and products – to an audience of several millions.

Show him the manufacturing and inspection areas, let him talk to your employees (brief them well beforehand). Be prepared to be interviewed yourself and, if you know that you are not up to it, be sensible and put forward a spokesperson who is. There's no point in making an idiot of yourself in front of all those people; it will quickly do both your company and your own reputation more harm than good, so be big enough to admit it and play safe.

Above all, don't let the producer go away unfed. Film people, given the choice, are always more likely to want to film in a location in which they will be well fed than to go to a desert island for the day.

Also, it's amazing what you can find out about the whole TV world over lunch with someone on the inside. Among the griping about his boss and the declining standards (don't be too quick to agree) there may well be nuggets of information that will help either this story or a future one. Mention to him what else you are doing, briefly and casually, and remember to mention it again, a little less casually when you next meet.

Finally, there's the filming day, the day when chaos comes to your factory and all hope of normal operating goes out of the window. You must be prepared for this; you're trying to reach millions of people and you can't do that without investing in time and effort and resource. If you're not prepared to have everything disrupted, then don't even try for TV in the first place.

A few basic rules must be observed. Have coffee ready for the crew and at least one 'Liaison' person who's doing nothing else for the rest of the day but catering for their every need. He or she will spend all day smoothing the path: calming down the electricians, for example, when the crew plug into the canteen power points or create a surge which throws all the computer systems into confusion.

The liaison person should also have a good lunch prepared with staff to serve it who can miraculously spend all day waiting for the great event and then produce a piping hot spread at the drop of a hat two hours later than was originally scheduled. What's more, they must do it cheerfully; film crews instinctively know when a place isn't happy.

The crew usually consists of a cameraman, a sound man, a lighting man, sometimes a presenter, sometimes a Producer's Assistant and, of course, the producer himself, resplendent in his oldest sweater. The first three will be union members and this can be important. A Canadian film crew I was once escorting around BL's Longbridge factory was unceremoniously bundled out by the company's shop stewards because their union wasn't recognized in the UK. The major pitfall in this area is usually the electricians who are quite capable of sabotaging the whole show unless their rules are adhered to.

Make sure the filming areas and the people working there are clean. Nothing looks worse on TV then slovenly surroundings and people. Position company logos or publicity material strategically in the background by all means but do it subtly (before the crew arrives) and be prepared to see it taken down unceremoniously just before filming. TV prefers you to pay for advertising.

A good idea is to kit out all your employees with clean, new and highly identified overalls just before filming. It may cost a bit, but you probably need overalls anyway and a prominent company name or logo on an employee's clothes cannot be erased. If the producer objects, try claiming some obscure clause under the Health and Safety at Work Act; it's a sure thing that he'll know even less about it than you do.

Filming in a factory can be a nightmare. Crews always want to see something spectacular and often, certain processes which may have little, or nothing, to do with the story are filmed to add colour to the treatment. Veracity can take second place to visual effects and strong statement.

This can involve setting up manufacturing or processing operations purely for the cameras – with the consequent creation of mayhem in the production schedules.

When the new Metro factory at Longbridge was finally ready for production to begin and TV crews were let in, the robots were regarded as being the most photogenic things since the Daleks. Consequently, every TV crew – and there were a lot – wanted particular, spectacular welding processes to be run and re-run. This resulted in much repetition of a few processes and did nothing to speed up production of the Metro in advance of launch date. But it proved marvellously compulsive viewing and some of the footage is still re-run even now, ten years after it was shot. It's no longer new, but it's still just as spectacular and illustrative of automated welding processes. Nevertheless, the time and disruption involved caused many a headache in the production management areas during a critical run up to a make-or-break launch.

The importance of the interview
Because it shows a human aspect to any story, the interview

is often the most important aspect of the TV coverage, and is the single most crucial part of any radio treatment. If you are up to it and if your presence is relevant to the story, do it yourself. If, in our example, you have masterminded the new factory and seen it come to fruition, then certainly try to handle the interview yourself. If, on the other hand, your story is centred on an obscure piece of research and development which may have interesting side effects, then get someone who really knows what they're talking about to handle the technical aspects while you deal with the broader commercial issues.

The cardinal rule in any interview is to work out what you want to say in advance and say it during the interview irrespective of whatever else might be going on at the time. This ploy has stood generations of politicians in good stead and who are you to say they're wrong?

Some interview trainers will tell you to write down the three points that you wish to make before starting the interview and then concentrate hard on getting them in as the interview progresses. This is fine if you want to make three points; it's a bit silly if you only have two things to say.

A more helpful approach to an interview is that you will not have time to make more than two or three points properly; TV is so immediate that sixty seconds is a lot of air time. Even all the effort and disruption that has gone into your programme – resulting in, perhaps, twenty minutes of wild (that is, unedited) filming is unlikely to command more than one or two minutes when it's edited down. So, your ability to get over your points must be based on a succinct grasp of the major issues. Don't try to go into detail – there isn't time. Say what you have set out to say and then shut up. Let the pictures and the presenter's voice-over tell the rest of the story.

A rehearsal normally precedes an interview. This is the opportunity to establish with the interviewer exactly what you wish to say about the topic and to agree on a line of questioning. It is also the time at which you make clear your willingness, or otherwise, to cover aspects of the topic which you may be reluctant to discuss in public.

If, for example, sections of your new factory are on strike, or 'in dispute' during the launch day (as part of BL's Metro factory was at Longbridge while both BBC and ITV cameras were based in the plant recording such homely programmes as *Nationwide*) then you obviously keep off the subject of industrial relations.

Generally speaking, however, try not to limit the range of the interview too much. Not only do producers know far better than you what topics are of interest to their viewers, but a reluctance to discuss seemingly innocuous matters makes a producer wonder what you're hiding and begin to question other information. As with a journalist, the best policy is always honesty.

If, however, you really do find the interview straying into unacceptable areas (such as the private lives of your employees or the misfortunes of another company) then you are perfectly within your rights to point out that you have already indicated that you are not prepared to discuss this matter. Do it politely but firmly and do not be afraid to do it even if the interview is being broadcast live.

Try to avoid embarrassing the interviewer like this because it is neither comfortable in the bar afterwards nor conducive to getting your company covered again by the same TV outfit. But, if there is no alternative and if the interviewer insists on returning to areas of confidentiality, then do not hesitate.

Some interviewers are unscrupulous enough to adopt this practice from time to time as a means of creating more exciting TV or radio. Usually, they do it during recorded interviews to give you a chance to object, but some have been known to use the device during a live interview. Treatment like that you do not need twice, so make it quite clear that the interviewer has broken the agreement which existed between you and that you are not prepared to be manipulated. The chances are that he'll respect you all the more for it.

Appearance is all on the TV screen. It can belie or confirm your words, exaggerate any facial expression or physical fault, convey exactly what you wish to avoid or make you into a hero overnight.

If in doubt, play safe. Wear a smart, conventional suit and remember that white shirts can come out yellow on some TV cameras; pale blue is recommended instead and, in any case, goes better with the accepted 'uniform' of a dark blue suit. Be unconventional if you like, but remember that you must be twice as good a performer to get away with it. The British public is not fond of rebels in charge of business outfits and even Richard Branson's woolly jumpers can look clichéd.

In terms of stance, try to be interviewed in a relaxed environment – get away from the office desk as being too formal and constricting. Don't fold your arms – it's the classic defensive attitude – and don't make the old David Owen mistake of keeping your hands in your pockets all the time. Stand in a calm, relaxed attitude – the producer will usually help you here by finding a good background and rehearsing you a couple of times before going for the 'Take'.

Look alert and interested. It's your factory they're talking about, but don't look smug or self-satisfied and, although smiles are important to create the impression of openness and welcome, use them sparingly. Not only do they then appear more effective and spontaneous, but also they can too often turn into grimaces in front of the camera. Even if they don't, very few families want their sitting rooms filled with grinning idiots while they're eating tea. Try to look confident, relaxed and, above all, natural. Every actor and actress strives for the ultimate in natural behaviour while reading what can be extremely unnatural lines; you have the advantage over them in that you are speaking your own words, so look sincere about it.

Sincerity and naturalness are the two great qualities of the amateur interviewee; affectation and hysterical hyping of material the surest ways to ensure that your first interview is your last.

Be careful too about the funnies. It is extremely hard to be funny in front of an audience. It requires hard work, considerable experience and unwavering devotion – just look at an old Tony Hancock video or at one of the maniacal *Fawlty Towers* episodes.

Furthermore, it is even harder to be funny with your own words after one or two rehearsals. It may be hard to write funny scripts, unless you have the genius of a P. G. Wodehouse, but it is even harder to deliver them convincingly. The third-rate night club circuit is full of failed comedians who will bear out this point and the producer will not like the show to be taken over by an embarrassingly amateur comedian.

In summary, look sincere and natural, be brief but pithy and convey belief in, and enthusiasm for, your subject. If it's your own factory, company or product, you shouldn't have much trouble.

The radio interview
Radio interviews follow similar patterns to those on TV except, of course, that you needn't worry too much about the way you look. You also usually have a little more time in which to make your point and the luxury of being able to write down what you want to say and read it verbatim without your listening public suspecting. This method does not suit all speakers and most professional broadcasters wouldn't be seen dead stooping to such an elementary trick. But you are not as experienced as they are and are far more likely to forget to make one or two important points unless they are written down in front of you.

To the interviewer or presenter, too, the issue is less important. They spend all their working time talking over the air or on the screen; if they forget to make a particular point during an interview, it's not so very important – there'll be another one coming along quite soon. To you, it could be the difference between a full order book and a difficult bank balance, so it's worth remembering the points.

Generally speaking, spoken radio programmes exist on interviews and talks of one sort and another. Magazine programmes, like *Woman's Hour*, are a series of talks with various people interspersed with linking commentary and, perhaps, the odd piece of music.

These interviews take two forms; face to face over an interview table or 'down the line' over the telephone. The first are usually preferred by producers and interviewers alike, partly because they don't have to move out of the office and partly because they have more control over the technicalities of voice levels and sound mixes. Telephone lines are subject to all kinds of interference including complete and abrupt severance; they have the additional disadvantage of being cold in that you and the interviewer can't see each other and this makes creating an apparently natural conversation more difficult. There are usually, also, fewer opportunities, if indeed any, to rehearse beforehand.

Whichever version you are offered, preparation is all. As with a TV interview, try to work out the two or three main points you wish to make and make them clearly but in the context of the discussion. This can take a bit of practice. It is very easy to become sidetracked and to go off at all sorts of tangents; these may, in themselves, be interesting, but they are unlikely to further your argument very much and they take up airtime. This often means that your other major points will remain unshared with the listening public.

Voice control, too, is important. One of the most common faults with any form of public speaking, whether on the air or live to an audience, is 'line fade'. This is the term for that strange phenomenon which suggests to speakers that, provided they start the beginning of the sentence clearly, nobody really minds if the last few words are inaudible. Although radio and TV engineers will do their best to help your voice level at all times, even they cannot do much about a voice which fluctuates wildly. To a live audience, line fade is the single most common cause of disaster. So try to give all your words sufficient volume.

Don't be drawn into the trap of giving each word equal weight, however, because then you'll have no room for emphasis and your major points will sound exactly like your more mundane utterances. Enunciate clearly and remember that terms and phrases which are very familiar to you may be unknown to your audience, so slow down a little when you come to them and give them a certain weight.

At the same time, avoid jargon as much as possible. Nothing turns off an audience quite so quickly as a string of abbreviations that are meaningless or the insistence on using technical terms that are too specialized to have come into everyday life. The vocabulary of the listening public is not large – certainly not by comparison with those who broadcast to them – and, unless a word or phrase is reasonably widely understood, your producer will probably ask you to find a clearer and more accessible substitute.

A very senior manager within British Leyland was once undergoing public speaking training with a trainer who was probably a little inexperienced for the task. The senior manager was preparing specifically for a presentation to an external audience not versed in the ways of the motor industry and used a number of technical phrases, common in the industry but largely unknown elsewhere.

'I'm sorry,' said the trainer, 'but those are phrases which are too specialized for this audience. Can you find a simpler way of expressing it?'

'No.' said the senior manager. 'It's perfectly simple and they will know what I mean.'

'Well, I don't understand it,'replied the trainer.

'In that case,' said the senior manager, rapidly losing patience, 'you're a fool.'

'No, Mr X, it's you who are the fool for expecting people to understand your gobbledegook.'

History, mercifully, draws a veil over the exchanges of the next few minutes; but I don't think that trainer ever worked in BL again.

The radio tape

There has been a series of developments recently in the way in which you can approach radio stations with a ready prepared tape and this is worth considering if you have the time and money and, above all, the requirement to get at the radio audience.

The radio tape is, simply, a pre-recorded tape, professionally produced to broadcast quality, which is then sent around a number of radio stations with a covering note. Because you pay for its creation and production, you can also determine its content, and, to a certain extent, its treatment. The rules of professional radio must apply, however, if you expect it to stand a realistic chance of being used,so it can't be too much of a puff for your message.

Try to retain a semblance of balanced comment and remember that radio producers are under no obligation to use it. I was involved with a radio tape for the Festival of Thailand in which the festival organizers wanted to compress as much adulation of the country as was possible in twenty minutes. Several retakes later, the finished product bore some resemblance to a balanced view of the attractions of the Festival but had deleted the more obsequious aspects of the recording.

In the event, the tape was widely used especially on local radio stations which tend to be the main recipients of the pre-recorded tape.

Where to target

Your targets for radio and TV approaches are predominantly local, at least in the first instance. National TV, in particular, is not noted for its enthusiasm for amateur, PR approaches, although there are exceptions such as *Tomorrow's World* which do all they can to recognize the vast wealth of material which they are offered.

TV is relatively simple. In any area of the country you have the choice of BBC or the Independent station, both of whom will listen to suggestions from local people with genuine stories to tell.

Local radio is much the same in format but more approachable – perhaps because it has more air time to fill – and more fragmented in that there are more radio than TV stations. Again, there is the divide between BBC and Independent broadcasting although the type of programme is often quite different with, in newspaper terms, the BBC more inclined towards the quality and middle-of-the-road press and the Independents more aligned to the popular tabloids.

Wherever you live and work, however, there is a comprehensive broadcasting network in the area.

Local broadcasting centres are listed below. (Telephone numbers and addresses are listed in your local telephone directory.)

Television
BBC

BBC Television Centre in London, serving national and South-East requirements
BBC Scotland – Glasgow, Edinburgh and Aberdeen
BBC Wales – Cardiff
BBC Northern Ireland – Belfast
Major Network Production Centres in:
  Birmingham, Manchester, Bristol
Regional TV Stations in:
  Norwich, Newcastle Upon Tyne, Plymouth

Independents

Independent Broadcasting Authority (IBA) in London, together with Channel Four and Independent Television News (ITN).

Anglia Television, based in Norwich, with Regional News Centres in Chelmsford, Luton, Northampton and Peterborough.

Border Television, based in Carlisle and covering Southern Scotland, Cumbria, Isle of Man and North Northumberland.

Central Television, based in Birmingham and Nottingham and covering the Midlands.

Channel Television, based in Jersey and Guernsey to cover the Channel Islands.

Grampian Television, covering Northern Scotland from Aberdeen, Inverness, Dundee and Edinburgh.

Granada Television, based in Manchester and Liverpool to cover the North-West.

HTV covering Wales and the West of England from offices in Cardiff and Bristol.

London Weekend Television (LWT) covering the inner South-East as well as London.

Scottish Television covering Central Scotland from offices in Glasgow and Edinburgh.

Television South-West (TSW), covering South-West England from base in Plymouth with offices in Barnstaple, Bridport, Bristol and St Austell

TV-AM provides a national service to all stations for morning television, based in London.

TVS serves the South and South-East from bases in Southampton, Maidstone and London.

Thames Television covers West London and the Thames valley from a London base.

Tyne-Tees serves the North-East from a base in Newcastle Upon Tyne with offices in Middlesborough and Northallerton.

Ulster Television based in Belfast.

Yorkshire Television covering the Pennines to the coast from a base in Leeds with offices in Sheffield, Hull, Lincoln, Ripon and Grimsby.

Radio

BBC Radio is based in London and covers not just the UK but the rest of the world through its World Service. However, more use to most PR operators is the extensive network of local stations, each of which is named BBC Radio ---- which, between them, cover the country. They are:

Radio Bedfordshire – based in Luton
Radio Bristol
Radio Cambridgeshire – based in Cambridge
Radio Cleveland – based in Middlesbrough
Radio Cornwall – based in Truro
Radio Cumbria – based in Carlisle
Radio Derby
Radio Devon – based in Exeter
Radio Essex – based in Chelmsford
Radio Guernsey – based in St Peter Port
Radio Humberside – based in Hull
Radio Jersey – based in St Helier

Radio Kent – based in Chatham
Radio Lancashire – based in Blackburn
Radio Leeds
Radio Leicester
Radio Lincolnshire – based in Lincoln
Radio London
Radio Manchester
Radio Merseyside – based in Liverpool
Radio Newcastle
Radio Norfolk – based in Norwich
Radio Northampton
Radio Nottingham
Radio Oxford
Radio Sheffield
Radio Shropshire – based in Shrewsbury
Radio Solent – based in Southampton
Radio Stoke-on-Trent
Radio Sussex – based in Brighton
Radio WM – based in Birmingham
Radio York

At the time of writing, another eight stations are planned to open within a couple of years covering Suffolk, Warwickshire, Thames Valley, Surrey, Gloucestershire, Hereford and Worcester, Wiltshire and Dorset.

In Scotland, there are:

Radio Scotland – based in Glasgow, Edinburgh and
    Aberdeen
Radio Aberdeen
Radio Dundee
Radio nan Eilean (Radio of the Isles) – based in Stornoway
Radio Highland – based in Inverness
Radio Orkney – based in Kirkwall
Radio Shetland – based in Lerwick
Radio Solway – based in Dumfries

Radio Tweed – based in Selkirk

In Wales:

Radio Wales – based in Cardiff
Radio Cymru – Welsh language, also in Cardiff
Radio Clwyd – based in Mold
Radio Gwent – based in Cwmbran

In Northern Ireland:

Radio Ulster – based in Belfast
Radio Foyle – based in Londonderry

Independent radio comes under the aegis of the IBA and includes:

BRMB – Birmingham
Beacon Radio – Wolverhampton
Capital Radio – London
Chiltern Radio – Dunstable and Bedford
County Sound – Guildford
DevonAir Radio – Exeter and Torbay
Downtown Radio – Belfast
Essex Radio – Southend and Chelmsford
GWR – Swindon and Bristol
Hereward Radio – Peterborough and Northampton
Invicta Radio – Canterbury and Maidstone
LBC – London
Leicester Sound
Marcher Sound – Wrexham
Mercia Sound – Coventry
Metro Radio – Newcastle
Moray Firth Radio – Inverness
NorthSound Radio – Aberdeen
Ocean Sound – Fareham
Pennine Radio – Bradford

Piccadilly Radio – Manchester
Plymouth Sound
Radio Aire – Leeds
Radio Broadland – Norwich
Radio City – Liverpool
Radio Clyde – Glasgow
Radio Forth – Edinburgh
Radio Hallam – Sheffield
Radio Mercury – Crawley
Radio Orwell – Ipswich
Radio Tay – Dundee
Radio Tees – Stockton-on-Tees
Radio Trent – Nottingham
Radio 210 Thames Valley – Reading
Radio Victory – Portsmouth
Radio Wyvern – Worcester
Red Dragon Radio – Cardiff
Red Rose Radio – Preston
Saxon Radio – Bury St Edmunds
Severn Sound – Gloucester
Signal Radio – Stoke-on-Trent
Southern Sound Radio – Brighton
Swansea Sound
Two Counties Radio – Bournemouth
Viking Radio – Hull
West Sound – Ayr

So, wherever you live, there are likely to be at least two TV
and two radio stations serving your catchment area. The
golden rule is to make sure that your story is genuinely local
before making a pitch. It must involve people, places or
events within the broadcasting area. If you observe this rule,
the local broadcasters will usually be helpful and friendly –
although remember that many other people and organizations are trying to get coverage as well as you, and

competition for limited air time is fierce, especially on TV; radio is a little easier.

The future perfect

Much has been written during the last few years about various revolutions in broadcasting and these are certain to come within the next decade. Cable and satellite television have already made a limited appearance while the proliferation of radio stations owes much to both the foresight of the BBC and the growth of private enterprise in the broadcasting sector. Sponsored television, too, is likely to rear its head much more within the next three years and the whole broadcasting world is waiting to see what the government will do to traditional charters and licences when they lapse in the near future.

What does all this mean to the PR operator and the advertiser? Should you be forsaking the traditional TV and radio channels and concentrating on this vision of the future when deregulated broadcasting will bring us a choice of up to thirty TV channels and dozens of radio stations all piped to the home; when all languages, cultures, creeds and tastes will be fully catered for and when new frontiers of broadcasting will be drawn in technological realms which are, as yet, a dream.

At the moment, it means very little to most of us. Much preparatory work is being done and a few people are getting quite excited, but the reality is that there are quite enough outlets for your information already. Keep your eye on developments, naturally, but bear in mind the numerous failures in experimental broadcasting which have already occurred. Cable TV has been a commercial washout, mainly because the logistics and the cost are both horrendous.

Satellite TV has been promised in tones akin to the Second Coming for almost a decade, but is still having to wait until the European broadcasting restrictions are lifted before becoming competitive. Those who have witnessed the

horrors of sponsored broadcasting in the States – epito-
mized by semi-permanent soaps – are largely lukewarm
about the prospect of having them in the UK. Those who are
not are usually counting on making money out of the
practice.

One possible exception to this is Sky Channel which has
kicked off in the UK with an opening fanfare which is only
just being matched by the number of satellite dishes which
are sprouting up in the suburbs. There are opportunities
here to get in ahead of the game, particularly on the
advertising side where favourable rates are traditionally
offered early in the lifetime of a new medium. Do not expect
viewing figures to be large enough to make a major impact
on your sales, however, satellite is still feeling its way and
the true potential will not be seen for at least a couple of
years yet.

Another possible pointer for the future is community radio
which is exactly that, a radio station for a very limited
community. A friend of mine in the BBC put it very
succinctly 'A station serving an offshore Scottish island
staffed by a man and a goat.' Other examples are a City
service which gives financial information all day and a
Brixton station which predominantly broadcasts reggae
music.

So far, the IBA has licensed twenty-one stations throughout
the country, but more are likely to be created as the idea
catches on. Initial enthusiasm seems to have been tempered
by financial constraints but the principle is one which will
probably endure and community radio may become the
norm rather than the exception by the end of the century.
In a word, wait and see what happens and certainly don't
spend precious time, energy and money on ventures which
could still turn out to be pipe dreams. Video has wrought its
own revolution in viewing habits, certainly, but just try
sending a video press release to a TV station to see how
welcome it isn't. The world of broadcasting is used to

changing faster than most of the rest of us; when really major changes are coming, it'll be sure to tell us.

5 The media event and the product launch

Now we deal with the theatrical aspects of PR: the presentations, launches and events at which you can ram home the message with varying degrees of subtlety.

The resemblance of these events to a theatrical production can be uncanny. All the preparation, the writing of the scripts, the building of the set, the lighting, sound and projection, the rehearsing of the speakers, the attraction of the audience, the creation of the visual aids, the technical rehearsal, the dress rehearsal and, finally, the big moment when the real, live audience is sitting facing you expectantly and you've got the opportunity to really come up with the goods. Not only that, but the sense of anti-climax afterwards is as flat as though you had just left *The Mousetrap* after a forty year run and you had no idea what to do next.

But events of this nature do not run themselves. They need very hard work and great attention to detail if they are to achieve their objectives. So let's start right at the beginning by looking at the purpose of the exercise, defining the terms and then look at the chronological unfolding of a major event.

What are you trying to achieve?
Although this is a useful question in any context, it is

particularly relevant to a major event because the time, trouble and cost involved can be considerable.

Generally, a press launch or other event of this nature shows that your courting of the media is working and that some of them are interested enough in what you have to say to come along and hear you say it on your own ground. This in itself is quite an achievement because journalists seldom have time to leave their desks for longer than it takes to down a few lagers.

Of course, you may not be dealing with the press at all. You may need to influence a gathering of City analysts, a team of financial backers, a local government committee or a network of retailers. You may be launching a new product or service, opening a new plant or facility, announcing a major investment programme or asking for financial support to carry out a major scheme.

The principles remain the same. You have decided to invite into your premises, or to neutral territory, a body of guests which has it in its power to influence the future of your business. You have invited them to see for themselves something of what you do, to meet some of your colleagues and to receive a new understanding of your requirements in their context.

The objectives, then, arise from this situation. You need to:

1 *Attract the right audience*. Nothing is more depressing than to go to a great deal of trouble and expense only to find that you are presenting to the caretaker, a stray cat and your own secretary – who's typed your speech anyway and is heartily fed up with it.
2 *Make the audience feel welcome*. Asking your security guards not to frisk them all on entry might be helpful in this respect.
3 *Impress them with what you have to say*. It's your personal reputation which is on the line as well as that of

your company. You can't afford to make an idiot of yourself in front of people from whom you need co-operation and support.

4 *Ensure that they go away with the message with which you want them to go away* – not with their own ideas of what you are trying to do. These may have been preconceived or they may have been picked up during the exercise. Both are unhelpful to your cause.

The whole point of putting yourself out in this way is to convince them that the way in which you see the situation is the right interpretation of the company's position and prospects. It is your interpretation and strategy which is going to ensure the company's successful future – so far as anything can.

So, let's look at these requirements in turn and try to establish a few ground rules which will help the event to go off with a successful swing.

Attracting the right audience

This is an exercise related closely to the basic media research which we have already looked at. The ground rules are simple: aim for those journalists who are – or who could be – genuinely interested in your story. Try to avoid the temptation to fill the place with friends, family, hangers-on and free loaders just to make up the numbers. Quality counts much more than quantity, although speaking to an almost empty room can be a salutary experience.

Question, therefore, whether you really need an event at all. The acid question is, are you going to get any greater coverage than you would if you simply produced a good quality press pack and circulated it to those journalists whom you know are interested in your affairs and products? Very often, the honest answer is 'No.'

There is, however, rather more to it than that. There are many other reasons why you should think about a press event if a suitable excuse offers itself.

One is that it is an excellent method of finding out exactly who is interested in you to the extent that they are prepared to leave their desks and come to see you. Another is that it is a way of creating the opportunity to influence one or more leading journalists without making the effort seem unduly forced. You have something to say that they would like to know about, and that is a very natural and proper channel of discourse between you.

It's also one which you can exploit to a certain degree by giving the journalists a full background briefing. This achieves two things:

1　It ensures they know the business context in which you are launching your new product.
2　It tempts them to give you rather more editorial coverage than they would otherwise be able to justify to their editor on the basis that the story is about the industry's background illustrated with your new development.

Nevertheless, if you've set your heart on having an event, you've got to make sure it's a success – and the first measure of this is whether you get the number of bums on seats. The second is whether the quality of those bums is of the right level – even if in the heat of the last minute arrangements, the temptation is to settle for quantity.

So, go through your press lists, go through your file of press cuttings to see who else is writing on related topics and who might be interested in attending. Go through your list of important contacts to see whether they will have access to any other journalists who should be invited.

Sometimes, press guests are mixed with other guests: suppliers, for instance, or dealers. This is almost always a serious mistake. For a start, other audiences require other messages and you can't afford to start diluting your messages to cater for different groups in the same room at once. It is neither professional nor successful.

If you want to present to your dealers – and it's usually a good idea - then do so with pleasure, but don't do it when the press are there. If you do, you'll run the risk of washing dirty linen in a glare of embarrassing publicity, with dealers seizing upon their unaccustomed limelight to demand another 2 per cent on the margin or protesting that they can't sell the inferior quality goods with which you're supplying them.

It matters not a whit that they are wrong or that you lace their bubbly with powdered glass at lunchtime; the damage has already been done and you may well find yourself with far more unwelcome publicity than you imagined staring at you out of the papers the next day. We're all human and there's nothing most journalists like more than a good private row that they can write up – as the Royal family would probably testify.

Second, journalists are arrogant enough to assume that they are a sufficiently influential sector of society to warrant a special event to themselves – and they are right. They don't usually mind sharing the stage with other publications (although even this rule has its exceptions) but they take considerable umbrage at being asked to tag along with a non-journalist audience, especially if it involves listening to a sales or marketing presentation – anathema to many journalists. This umbrage has some justification. Journalists are objective, impartial observers who like to have the opportunity to make up their own minds. In any case, you're either going to do the job properly or else it's not worth doing.

There's nothing to stop you taking advantage of the presentation arrangements for other audience sectors, though. That's simply prudent, cost-effective marketing.

In 1982, for example, Freight Rover launched the new Sherpa range of vans to replace a product which had been around since the early 1950s. As it was also the first new product from a newly identified and established company, albeit one still within the BL empire, it was clearly a major milestone in that company's fortunes.

Accordingly, we took one of the halls at the National Exhibition Centre near Birmingham – a hall which, at first sight, looked as though it could comfortably accommodate most of the aircraft flying in the Western world.

There were two major audiences: dealers and media. There were several hundred dealers and each one was encouraged to send as many representatives as possible. There were only about fifty journalists who could be remotely counted as relevant, but the way in which they reported the new vehicle was the key to its fortunes.

So, we built a massive set which split in two down the middle, commissioned a film, created a whole marketing launch presentation (dealing with product specifications, pricing strategy, vehicle derivatives and marketing support spend), put about twenty Sherpas on display behind the stage like a motor show, and wrote presentations for all the key people: the Managing Director, the Director of Product Planning, the Sales Director and the Dealer Services Manager – as well as the Director of Communications and Public Affairs.

The presentation set the new product in its business context, extoled its engineering virtues and lauded its abilities to create showroom traffic for the dealers. Core parts of the presentation were given to all audiences but others were omitted for different audiences.

Dealers and press never met. They stayed at different hotels on different days, but the core of the presentation was the same for all. Elements written especially for the dealers (concerning marketing strategy and back up cost) were omitted for the press.

It is certainly true to say that the whole show was more effective than most van launches of its time. Although the heyday of the laser had not yet arrived, dry ice and strobe lighting had and the dividing stage was a revelation.

Indeed at one point it was a revelation to me. I was concluding the press presentation on the first night and made the cardinal error of ad libbing a few lines away from the autocue. The dry ice began to rise about my legs and, while I was still making my final comments, the stage began to divide. This would not have mattered too much except that I was standing with one foot on each side of the dividing line – a fact of which nobody but I was aware. I narrowly avoided yelping and leaping off the stage before side stepping with what I hoped was a nonchalant ease. Colleagues afterwards told me that I looked like a startled horse – I think they were trying to be kind.

Making your visitors welcome

Good, old fashioned courtesy is still one of the main foundations of good PR. Maybe it's because courtesy has gone out of fashion to an alarming extent that it's now more of a novelty than it used to be; maybe it's simply that courtesy is appreciated wherever and whenever it's found. Whatever the reason, it can work wonders in bringing round observers to your point of view.

Courtesy starts before your visitors arrive. It starts with the issuing of the invitations which set out a number of salient facts.

1 What is happening and why
2 Where and when it's happening
3 Why it will be of interest to the recipient of the invitation letter

By including this information you whet the appetite with indication of the importance of the exercise. You also make the recipient realize that he or she has been selected from a large number of similarly placed people to sample the whole package of communications that you are putting on show. In this sense, they are privileged, and that starts off the relationship on a sound and mutually appreciative footing.

A follow-up call, preferably from your secretary, to check that the guest has received the invitation, and realizes its significance, also gives you the opportunity to discover whether the guest is coming. This makes easier the tasks of planning seating and catering. It is also generally appreciated if you send directions to the venue, especially if the guests are coming by car and you are a bit off the beaten track.

Transport

Sometimes, for sizable parties coming to, say, a new factory opening, it pays to negotiate with British Rail for a special train or to lay on coaches or minibuses to meet guests at the nearest mainline station. This is particularly useful if you are working outside the South East and expecting, or hoping for, guests from London whose choice of trains is limited.

For really important guests, chauffeur driven cars (of a reasonable quality such as Granadas or Senators) are often used. Far from being over the top, this is an increasingly popular way in which to subtly state the importance which you place upon the attendance of your guests. In some country areas, or in the centre of London, it is also often the most practical method of transport. What can be even more important, it also ensures that you allow guests to leave on time to catch a vital train or plane home.

Arrival

It is essential that your guests are checked in and registered, partly because you don't want unidentified people wandering around your premises and partly because you want to retain a written record of your guests after they've gone as a basis for follow-up contact and as a core invitation list for the next event.

In any case, it adds to the professionalism of the visit and this sticks in the mind of the visitors.

A small table with one or two secretaries ticking off names against a visitors' book and handing out lapel badges is usually the best method. Badges are very useful because they prevent most of the awkwardness of gatherings in which nobody knows or remembers who anybody else is.

In addition, one or two receiving hosts hovering around the table ensure that guests are greeted with an invitation to coffee or drinks. This also stops the guests hanging round the reception table and preventing the registering of others.

Impress your guests with what you have to say
This is important, but equally important is the way in which you say it. Shakespeare wrote very few original plots but his versions of well-known stories are remembered when all others are not. All the novels in the world have already been written; new titles which keep appearing are simply new versions of old stories.

Similarly, it is unlikely that you have got anything really original to say. You may have a new product or a new method of producing one, but it is likely to be a variation on a theme rather than a completely new departure. Even if you think it's brand new, the journalists who scan the whole of your industry sector are likely to have seen or heard of something similar before. You must, therefore, be careful not to overstate its merits.

One of Austin Rover's major errors of the 1980s, for example, was to overstate the merits of the Austin Maestro, a car generally regarded by the motoring media as 'lack-lustre' even at its introduction, and one which was palpably not as advanced as much of the competition. Senior management's insistence on hyping an inferior product caused considerable and lasting damage to the reputation of both the car and the company in the motoring and motor industry press. The general media attitude was that management must think the press fools to believe their claims.

So, consider carefully what you *need* to say and, only then what you *want* to say:

1 For instance, it is useful to give some background to your company and its strengths and positioning before you launch the product itself. A new development from a small company is more likely to win respect than the same development from a large outfit with a massive research department of whom constant innovation is expected. So outline the size, growth and philosophy of your operation, not exhaustively – that will bore your audience, which is the ultimate discourtesy – but in a maximum of ten minutes.

2 Then go on to the background to the new product itself: why it is necessary or desirable, what sparked off the concept and – briefly - how it was developed. Make sure that you present it as a customer-led initiative. Sales- or operations-led developments cannot be justified so strongly or presented as being as useful or beneficial to the community. In other words, greater profit, growth or investment are not reasons for introducing new product as far as most of the press is concerned – although the *Financial Times* will be more sympathetic to this approach than most. What does command 'brownie points' is the development of something useful to society or to a section of it. Even the creation or preservation of jobs no longer has the emotive pull which it used to when unemployment was soaring over the three million mark and the prospects of an upturn were bleak. Job creation is still a useful side story to your new product – job preservation less so because it's less emotive at the end of the 1980s – but that's all that these are: angles to add into the general mix from which your new product is to be launched.

3 Now that you've whetted the appetite you are ready to reveal the new product. Try to do so in a professional way. Don't just leave a few lying about for the journalists to fall over; organize a proper 'reveal' with as much theatre as you think the audience will stand. For large

products, a specially built set is sometimes useful, and this enables you to arrange proper lighting, projection and sound as well as reveal curtains or other drapes. Smaller products too can often benefit from the semi-theatrical background, the whole purpose of which is to create an effect which will be left in the minds of the audience long after they've left your premises.

Retention of image (as the process is called) can go a long way to secure a favourable press for some considerable time to come. It shows that you believe in the product enough to support it and that you are being professional about the way in which you are launching and marketing it. It also demonstrates commitment and support to the developers and workforce involved and, if appropriate, to the dealer network through which you are expecting to sell it.

You may round off with an indication of the kind of marketing approach which you are going to take, but, unless you're presenting to the marketing press only, keep this brief and, if in doubt, omit it altogether. Its value is to demonstrate the way in which the marketing messages summarize all the things that you have been claiming for the product; the disadvantage can be that the journalists think that they are sitting through a marketing presentation which is irrelevant to them.

4 At the end of the presentations it is essential to provide the opportunity for the journalists to see, try or somehow experience the product for themselves. This is easy if you're in the food and drink industry, much more difficult if you've just launched a new type of concrete building material. Nevertheless, try to arrange at least an exhibition of its virtues and properties. The journalists may not understand it when they see it but at least they are more likely to be impressed by a graphic demonstration of its worth, as indeed are most audiences.

If your event is being held in the factory which also makes your new product, a visit to the production lines – or those bits of it which are relevant, respectable, interesting and hi tech – is a useful way of adding to the educational process. It also gives you a breather before the guests come back for lunch.

Ensure though that the place is clean and reasonably tidy, that the graffiti is removed along with the more lurid pin ups and that your workforce:

1 Knows what's happening and why.
2 Knows what's expected of them in terms of demonstrations and general behaviour.
3 Is wearing clean overalls with the company name on them.
4 Has been invited to take part in a similar launch presentation prior to that aimed at the journalists. This will not only fix the new product's importance firmly in the minds of your workforce, in terms of job security and opportunity, but ensure also that they realize the importance of cultivating good media reaction at launch stage.

One way of demonstrating this is to equate sales levels with production levels and thus to pay and bonus levels – it concentrates the mind wonderfully. Moreover, a committed workforce can do more good in an ambassadorial role than all your marketing staff put together. Their sentiments are less clouded with marketing speak and more likely to be sincerely expressed and received.

Now let's relax...
After all this is over, bring on the refreshments – or, at least, invite the journalists into the room where the refreshments are laid out. It doesn't need to be lavish – indeed, that can be counterproductive – but it should include the normal contents of a journalist lunch – good, straightforward food

with decent, but not expensive, wine and beer and soft drinks as an option. Unless it's a formal dinner, keep off spirits; they are not appreciated, are more likely to be abused and are more expensive.

Lunches are easier and less intimidating if they are served in buffet form. Sit-down meals tend to be hard work and too time consuming for most journalists. Don't forget that, although you've set aside the day for this exercise – and you must – the journalists probably have another two or three stories to cover that day and do not want only one to take up most of their working time.

This refreshment break can be the most important part of the whole day. It is here that the clever journalist will take you or a senior manager aside and try to worm out more than is in the press pack. This can be very beneficial, if you remember the principles of giving interviews, or it can be disastrous if you or your manager are caught off guard. For this reason, it is a good rule to allow only your guests to take alcohol – after they've all gone, you can open another bottle and share it with your managers because only then will you, and they, have earned it.

Allow time for a question and answer session at the end of your presentation by all means – you'll probably get a few questions anyway – but the good journalists will keep quiet and tackle you, or somebody else, over lunch.

How you react to this is likely to dictate the kind of coverage that you eventually receive, or, indeed, whether you receive any coverage at all. So, do not relax your guard until the last guest has left and do *not* let inexperienced managers loose at lunch.

Indeed, do not let anybody loose without a full briefing beforehand: who is coming, what their views may be, what kind of articles they write, what sort of editorial policy their publications adopt, whether they are known to be politically biased and whether they are known to be trouble stirrers. The more important your company, the more important it is that you get this homework right in advance; to leave it to the day can be fatal.

Above all, ensure that the journalists go away with the message you want them to have.

How to present
We've talked glibly of 'presenting' but what do we mean and how do you go about it?

Most presentations set out with the aim of presenting a professionally constructed message, or series of messages, to a given audience. It follows, therefore, that they should look as professional as possible without going over the top and employing brass bands at half time. There are a few elements which are widely perceived to add professionalism and it's worth considering some of them in any presentation you have to make.

Scripting
Very few people can guarantee to give an impressive presentation each time they stand up. All sorts of external factors get in the way and affect the performance – from indigestion to worrying about last week's sales figures.

So, give yourself a chance and minimize the risks. Prepare what you're going to say very thoroughly, and discuss it with your senior management. Make sure that you haven't forgotten anything and that you're expressing the facts in the best possible way. This often means applying the most positive interpretation to the facts without altering them or losing sight of honesty, integrity or truth.

Marshal your arguments as logically as you can; make sure that you introduce the topics in a sensible order with a flow of reason that can be understood by an audience which does not have your insight into the subject.

The cardinal rule is to have a beginning, a middle and an end. The beginning, the *introduction*, should set out your whole argument in a nutshell of not more than two or three sentences and describe what you are going to say. The middle *develops your argument* and *adds as much detail as you need* – but not enough to turn off your audience. The end *restates your case* in a shortened form so that anybody coming in for the last minute would understand what you are saying.

This classic formula works when many other, more fancy or ambitious attempts do not. It has the merit of being direct, open and succinct. The average attention span of a moderately well-educated audience is less than twenty minutes – and that's not long once you've stood up and started to talk.

Speaking notes

There are three main methods of remembering what you are going to say: notes, verbatim scripts and luck. As a senior manager, you should discount the last one. Standing up without any notes at all and no visual aids to jog the memory is not a professional way to go about making a presentation. It is also a discourtesy to your audience to ramble off at a tangent or to try desperately to remember what you were going to say next. It is counterproductive in that your audience either becomes bored and stops listening or, even worse, treats you as an object of ridicule and declines any future invitations.

Whether you should use notes or a verbatim script is a matter for your own experience and confidence in public speaking. There is no right or wrong answer. People prefer one to the other depending upon their experience and how fluent they feel in talking about their subject.

The key is to be as natural as possible. Don't force things, don't try to be too funny – it's very difficult to bring off – and above all, keep it short. Don't use six words where one will do and don't use long words and technical terms for the sake of them. You can usually find a simpler and better way of saying things if you think about it for a bit. You can't assume that your audience knows much, if anything, about your subject. All you can assume is that, by their very presence, they are prepared to listen to what you've got to say.

If you are reading verbatim, make sure you have a good solid lectern or podium on which to rest your sheets of paper. Nothing looks more amateurish than having a sheaf of unruly papers which keep fluttering and rustling and probably getting mixed up.

If it's a large room and the acoustics are not good, use a microphone or public address system. If you are going to the expense of a full PA set, you may think about an autocue: a clever piece of perspex in which you can see your words scrolling up as you read them while they remain invisible to the audience (a device used by news readers on television).

Unfortunately, most of us are not experienced television news readers and cannot assume a practised, natural air when confronted with the things. Consequently, they tend to make normal speakers wooden and wooden speakers unbearable. You are so busy following the words that you lose all thought of what you are saying or the way in which you are saying it. Expression and emphasis go by the board and, if the autocue operator (who's sitting behind a curtain rolling the script up the machine by hand) makes a mistake or hasn't got the latest changes to your script, you're completely sunk.

Your mind mysteriously refuses to work and your thoughts simply will not focus on what you were going to say next. If you're speaking from notes, you're thinking all the time about what you're saying and can recover from the odd aberration far more easily.

Visual aids
Try to make your material more interesting and more understandable by using as many visual aids as possible.

Essentially, this means drawing pictures for the audience to look at while you describe some of the finer points of detail and point out the salient features.

It also makes the presentation easier for you because you have a visual image of what you're talking about in front of you acting as an aide memoire, and can refer to points of detail in the reasonable expectation that your audience will be able to follow you.

There are all sorts of visual aids: simple flip charts, overhead slides, projected 35 mm slides, tape slides, video and film inserts. They all have in common the fact that they communicate information pictorially – the form in which it is easier to assimilate and easier to retain.

Most business and financial information lends itself to slides quite easily (bar charts, graphs, matrices and so on) and the best method of projection is usually the 35 mm slide. Overhead slides often look messy and can be invisible from the back of the room, and flip charts are a bit home-made for all but internal presentations.

Moving footage, whether on film or video, is excellent for truly visual material but is often used as an excuse to make bad material more presentable. Many business videos do not need to be made at all, but the fashion and myth that you 'need a video' if you are to be taken seriously has gained much ground recently. Very often you don't need it and with prices ranging up to £2,000 per finished minute – if not more – it's an expensive way of keeping up with the Joneses. In any case, reproducing video to large audiences is not yet a technically perfect process and the quality of your tape when shown may well turn out to be disappointing.

Using a PA in conjunction with visual aids can be distracting. Whenever you turn to the screen, which is usually to one side of you, you automatically turn your voice projection away from the mike, thus rendering yourself inaudible to most of the room. Contact mikes which are clipped to your jacket can avoid this pitfall, although they can also take some getting used to.

Additionally, the slide may distract the audience from what you are saying or the audience may be so busy trying to read it that they stop listening to you.

Another distraction is the press kit or copy of your speeches given out in advance – a fatal mistake. Most of your audience will ignore your presentation and write their story from the hand-outs as you are laboriously reading your golden words. Others will, even more blatantly, ring through a story from your nearest phone or look very put out when you tell them there isn't a phone anywhere near – another pretext for leaving early. Make sure that your press pack is handed out *after* all the presentations have been completed but before question time so that they can be used to prompt questions.

The key to successful presentations, therefore, is to keep a balance: use as much in the way of visual aids and technical assistance as you need to keep the presentation fresh and appealing, but stop short of letting technical trickery take over – it can too easily turn to cliché and gimmickry. Be brief, honest and clear and you will probably earn more respect as a result – especially from hardened hacks who have seen most – or all – of it before.

Briefing the troops

Remember that the good journalist will always try to get an angle that nobody else has thought of and may well try to obtain information from a member of your staff without you knowing anything about it until the milk is spilt. Ensure, therefore, that all your staff are fully briefed with the answers to all likely, and most unlikely, questions. Anticipate points of potential embarrassment and work out credible and truthful answers in advance. Then circulate this question and answer (Q and A) document to all who may come into contact with the guests and threaten them with anything you like if they depart from the gospel.

This is known, quaintly in view of its limitation of the truth, as 'Reading from the same hymn sheet' and can be a godsend in the face of probing journalism.

The Q and A will also help to ensure that your guests go away with the message you want them to have, not the message they want to have.

Key messages

Everything we've discussed is aimed at influencing the journalist to adopt your point of view on given facts: the selection of those facts, the method of presentation, the interpretation of stated data and the careful creation of a background conducive to belief in your point of view.

An essential stage of preparation is to decide on two or three key messages and write them down as briefly and simply as possible. They may, for instance, be 'investment', 'quality' and 'growth' – not startlingly original but very typical of the kind of impression a business often wants to make.

Then write your presentation and, when you're satisfied with it, re-read it in the light of these three key messages. Does it reflect them? More, does it seize every opportunity to hammer them home, either directly or more subtly? Is it all relevant to those themes? Does the overall quality of the presentation and the event (script, visual aids, press pack and hospitality) reflect a company which has invested, is improving quality and increasing sales? Is there a false note anywhere, anything which is not in keeping with what you're trying to say? If there is, a journalist will sniff it out immediately and then question the validity of the rest of the information he or she's been given, maybe even the integrity of those who gave it.

Keep your key messages with you the whole time. Have them framed and mounted on the office wall if that helps you to remember them, but never lose sight of them. Unless you're committed to them and constantly conversant with them, you can't hope to convince anyone, least of all a journalist, that you are serious about them. And if you aren't serious about them, you can't very well expect any of your employees to put them into operation with any degree of commitment.

The evaluation

After the event it's only prudent to attempt to make some evaluation of its success. Comments made by the journalists on the day are often the best – and certainly the most immediate – form of feedback and it's useful to compare notes with all the other hosts as soon as the last guest has left. That way you can judge the overall impression, what was liked, what was regarded with scepticism, what was seen as the most newsworthy angle and so on. This is all very valuable in assessing the impact you have made, where the gaps are and what you need to do to correct wrong impressions.

The second stage is to monitor the resulting coverage to see, first of all, if the journalists understood what you were telling them, second, whether what they wrote supports their oral feedback to you – it usually will – and, third, what they really think of your operation based on the information that you created and supplied.

Try not to place too much emphasis on the media coverage however. It is not the only achievement of the exercise by any means. You have built bridges simply by meeting and talking to these journalists – and remember to *listen* to what they have to say as well as to tell them what you have to say. They often have a broader perspective of your business sector than you can ever have and you may well learn something useful.

You have built bridges. You can now develop the relationships. You've got a better idea of who really is influential and who is more lightweight; you know who to approach next time and who to treat as a priority. You may wish to invite one or two to lunch individually and just use the time to air topics on the industry. That way, both parties will learn and move closer to a mutually useful relationship based on respect and professionalism. And, if you have a few tasty titbits up your sleeve, you'll more than likely get a good story out of it as well, one that is exclusive to the publication for which the journalist writes.

So, treat the media event as a diplomatic mission, one which observes all the old-fashioned courtesies but which also contains a solid, professional and relevant basis of key messages presented convincingly to key audiences. Coverage is jam on the bread and butter; what you've really gained is recognition as a serious competitor in your business field – and that's something which cannot be bought.

6   Community relations

That old chestnut 'You get out what you put in' is particularly true of community life – both in business and social terms.

By simply existing, you and your business both have a role in your local community. You may have your roots there too, and this can be very advantageous in developing your business.

There will be two distinct roles: that occupied by your business and that occupied by you, yourself. They will exist in different circles of contacts, circles which may touch only at the edges or may be closely intertwined.

Your business may be part of the Chamber of Commerce and the local branch of a national trade association, while you may be in your child's school Parent Teacher Association and the village cricket club. Nevertheless, these are four examples of contact circles through which you can extend your sphere of awareness and influence because you are participating more fully in the life of the community in all its aspects. By doing so, you can ensure that you create a greater knowledge of your business locally and, thus you also create greater potential for business development.

There are two major types of community which can affect your business; the social framework of your area and the business community itself. Included in the latter are the official and semi-official organizations and institutions which form the basis of all local business interests. The Chambers of Trade and Industry, for example, whose role it is to promote commercial life in a certain geographical area, provide a useful service for most businesses and especially for the small and medium-sized company.

But, by itself, membership of a Chamber or any other institution does not automatically bring benefits. You must invest in far more than the membership fee before you are likely to see much in the way of returns.

On another and more official level, local government has it in its power to be either very helpful or very awkward. To a certain extent, your own approach can influence which end of the stick the local council chooses to take.

Most local councils have a reputation for being less than helpful (or even downright obstructive) possibly because of a lack of commercial knowledge and experience, or possibly because their political beliefs include a suspicion of small and successful private enterprise. A lack of commercial experience, far from being a problem, can, of course, be an opportunity to educate the appropriate officers and councillors into a more business-like way of thinking. If you combine this by demonstrating your commitment to the community, much greater co-operation can often be obtained.

Then there is the social level, the voluntary and purely social groups which not only represent a proportion of the buying power in your area but who also exercise considerable – if unofficial – influence over others in the matter of choosing how much to spend where. Many small businesses have been made or broken on the strength of local gossip.

So what are these circles and who forms them? What influence can they have and how can you, in turn, influence them?

The types of local organization

First comes the business organization, which exists to help commercial interests in the area. Chambers of Commerce, Trade or Industry exist in most regions and are usually centred on a town or city. As well as the usual benefits of newsletters, central services (such as reference libraries, assistance with export initiatives and regular forums in which to learn and make your opinion known), these Chambers also often act as unofficial recommenders of goods and services not only to their own membership but to the local market as a whole. It follows, therefore, that most members will try to do business with one another rather than with outsiders.

Then there are societies which nominally exist for other purposes but which in fact have a large element of mutual benefit in their make up. Freemasons have, rightly or wrongly, attracted this kind of image over the years – although it never seemed to do my father any noticeable good and he was a member for nearly twenty years.

Rotarians and Round Tablers were set up to raise money for charity, which they do, but they also manage to learn a good deal about each other's businesses on the way. More obscure clans like the Ancient Order of Water Rats and the Royal Order of the Moose seem to be more secretive about their activities (although this may be a natural result of their scarcity), but membership may often be business-based and the emphasis of the societies remains rooted in that context.

Moving away from the business and semi-business sectors, there are hundreds of other kinds of organization which offer contact points with the local community at large and most of them are worth cultivating. School-based societies like PTAs, Friends groups (usually there to help raise funds) and, more officially, Boards of Governors, will obviously be well worth joining if your business is in any way involved in the supply of educational material or services. Even if it isn't, these groups form the basis of a new network of contacts, some of which may one day prove rewarding.

Church-based societies are legion: Women's Institutes, Mothers Unions, choirs, Parochial Church Councils (PCCs), youth groups, Guides, Scouts, Brownies, Cubs, Boys' Brigade, bellringers, Parish Councils and many more. They are all useful entry points into the community and, in particular, to that section of the community which unofficially assesses consumer value. Parish Councils or District Councils are also useful pressure groups to influence if you want planning permission – or if you don't want somebody else to have planning permission.

Membership is based on election but there are more seats than candidates on many councils, making the electoral process comparatively painless. Once elected, few councillors find they are overworked – unless by choice – although their influence over such issues as planning applications, fixing the rating levels and local development plans can be considerable.

Local sports clubs (for an ever increasing range of sporting and leisure activities) give access to active and leisure markets, both sectors which are growing all the time. Evening classes and arts and recreational societies (such as drama, music, folk dance, local history groups and so on) provide another way in to target and influence various sectors of the community.

How the neighbourhood can help you

What all these groups, and many others too numerous to mention, have in common is the ability to benefit your business and they do so in several ways.

First, there is the simple and obvious factor of meeting more people and organizations in the area, some of whom may one day want to buy your service or product rather than patronize your competitors. Make an effort to make a favourable impression and you may well find your local sales increase in proportion.

Second, there is the possibility of developing contacts throughout a more business-based circle, contacts which can materially help to further your business. Examples would be a company with complementary skills and needs or one who can supply your raw material at better rates or quality levels than you can buy elsewhere.

But, third, less obviously and most importantly in the PR context, there is the opportunity to raise your profile generally within the local community: the opportunity to make your name – and that of your company – synonymous with the product or service that you offer. This is a necessary precursor to the process of making your business so well known in the locality that it becomes the natural place to which potential customers will come when they need that product or service.

There are two intertwined aspects to this process of raising the awareness level of your business. The first is to raise your company's profile in a straightforward fashion to make it widely known in the region for what it does or for what it provides. This is the elementary level of awareness not necessarily extending to appreciation which has been demonstrated for centuries by shop fronts and delivery vans. Boots the Chemist is one of the purest examples of this process. The three words tell you who does what in the simplest form possible – something for which advertising agencies can strive fruitlessly for years.

The second, which can be proportionately beneficial, is to raise your own personal profile to a level commensurate with a respectable and successful standing in society. Thus, by associating your company with your personal standing and success you can greatly assist the growth of your business. If, for example, you run a golf club manufacturing company and you play off an impressive handicap on all the local golf courses, win tournaments and generally feature large in the local golf life, you are likely to find that demand for your clubs is considerably greater than it would otherwise be.

One of the best ways to acquire respectability for your business, therefore, is to acquire respectability for yourself. If you can become known as being an expert on some aspect of your business then you can begin to count on people's respect and ultimately, their support and commercial commitment.

One of the achievements of many successful leaders of business is that they have become known for their knowledge of certain sectors or industries and that reputation has done their companies and other business interests no harm at all.

Yet, they all started somewhere. Each self-made business-man or woman started their business in a small geographical area. Each one of them made it a priority to acquire a reputation for being good at – or knowledgeable about – something within a fairly small catchment area before moving further afield to set the world on fire. And most of them took a pro-active role in the local community as part of this process.

Approaching the community

So, how do you go about becoming the local authority on your chosen subject or in your sphere of activity? How do you sell yourself to a community?

Clearly, the first stage is to become something of a self-publicist who attracts attention through a variety of contributions to different parts of the local community. Address meetings on topics on which you have knowledge, interest and strong opinions, write letters to the local newspapers pointing out aspects of events which they have omitted to cover or adding to stories they have already run.

Join action groups dedicated to a cause in which you believe or, better still, start one yourself. Bob Geldof will probably be remembered by future generations not as a singer but as the architect of Ethiopian famine relief.

Play a prominent part in local politics and government – but make sure that your own ambition coincides with and does not conflict with that of your chosen political party.

Write books on your speciality and have them reviewed locally – a sure way of getting into the local papers.

Adjudicate in local competitions of all sorts, from judging the roses at the Flower Show to the beauty contest in the night club.

Preferably, get yourself on to local TV and radio so that you achieve the maximum impact in the broadcasting area. (Most of the activities mentioned will help to make this easier to achieve.) Once you've got this far, you become known not just for your original expertise but through this as a sort of minor celebrity – at which time people actively want to do business with you because it means that they can talk about knowing you.

How then do you switch the focus to your company and business interests to ensure that they share in the rewards? To a certain extent, you don't. You are the one who has become well known and you, therefore, are the person people want to meet. What you must do is to associate yourself very strongly with the local activities of your business; become the company spokesperson and use the office to publicly embrace issues far wider than those of your company.

Once you've established this association, it is a relatively simple matter of promoting the company locally and there are a number of ways of achieving this.

One of the best is through the good offices of our old friends the local media. They are usually keen to cover stories with a local content especially if you can inject an element of human interest: an employee who has triplets is a good picture story, even better if he happens to be male.

Weddings, retirements, sporting achievements, unusual hobbies are all good local paper fodder.

But this time the interest is – or should be – more focused on your business. So, you need to promote that business or its people as playing an active part in the local community. Participation in local affairs of all kinds is one way not just to get into people's good books but also to get into the media good books.

Support a local fund raising effort for charity, organize some sort of local event or competition, reclaim derelict land that your company owns and allocate some of it to local uses. Embark upon an environmentally useful scheme that improves the lives of local people – tree planting, for example, or sponsoring a local environmental volunteer group. Create jobs. Every national story to do with business investment or decline usually has an interest in the number of jobs created or destroyed and the local media interest is, naturally, even stronger.

Above all, be seen to be taking an interest in the affairs of the local community. It is not enough to participate; you have to be *seen* to participate. Every time you do something which even remotely affects the area in which your business has its being, tell the papers and the radio stations. They may not use it the first time or even the second; but they will appreciate being told and get used to the fact that somebody is telling them about what's going on. Sooner or later, they will use something that you send them and then you have the opportunity to build really strong and lasting links.

Immediately you, or if you wish to delegate the task, the manager who carries out this policy, become a local celebrity you acquire a profile in the community and from that beginning the nature of your local role can change rapidly.

You may not wish to have your private life invaded. You may think that you work hard enough at the office without having to assume a high public profile when you're supposed to be relaxing. In this, you have a point, although many successful business people would argue that you can never afford to relax off duty. There is a cliché in the PR consultancy world that you 'can't afford to have an off day' and there is some truth in this remark. It all depends on how much success you want and how much you and your family can handle, what you enjoy doing in your spare time and how much influence over your business and personal destiny the local community can have.

Do not underrate this last point. Just because you export all your production to Saudi Arabia does not mean that your local community has nothing to do with your company's success. You need employees. You may need planning permission for an extension. You may need to buy new vehicles, plant or equipment. You may want to challenge your rates bill. All these activities take place within a relatively small local arena despite the nature of the product or the destination to which it is shipped.

It follows that your attention needs to be given to this arena and not just at the time when you need the help of the local community to achieve something. As with media relations, it is important to build up a rapport with all sorts of local opinion factions so that, when you do want their help, it is more likely to be forthcoming.

Furthermore, all this activity may not be carried out where you live. If your company is situated miles away from your home, you have the classic dichotomy. Most of your socializing will take place outside the arena of your business activity – and this is especially true in the South-East where comparatively few business people now live in central London.

What is also important is the way in which the community close to the company's premises think about the firm. What your local village thinks about you is important to you but may not affect the fortunes of your company very much.

What the community local to your business thinks about you as an employer, a property developer, a landlord, or an entrepreneur matters very much. It can affect the ease or difficulty with which you can recruit staff, build new premises, appeal against the rates and purchase goods and services.

You either have a good reputation in business or you do not. If you do not, you cannot afford to relax. If you don't know whether you do or not, you still can't afford to relax. Only when you are so successful that there is nothing that can possibly threaten your business base can you afford the luxury of relaxing – very few businesses are in that position.

The community campaign

Addressing meetings of all kinds is an excellent way of influencing the local community. You may be voted onto a local committee or organization, in which case you need to be seen to be contributing effectively to its business. Or you may simply be attending as an interested party. Either way, you need to be able to contribute effectively to meetings without forgetting that the other people present are not necessarily well disposed towards you to start with. They may not know anything about you or your business, or they may have preconceptions about both you and your company. In some cases they may feel hostility towards you over a sensitive local issue such as a planning application.

This is when PR can do much to correct their opinions, when it can greatly help to educate and inform them so that they begin to see the situation from your point of view. It may not solve the differences, but it is likely to create a climate of opinion in which the two sides can draw closer together so that the ultimate solution is easier.

A large chemical company with a factory in the North West used to have considerable local difficulties. Pollution from its chimneys was so bad that, at one stage, it even burned holes in the washing left out on the lines by the local housewives. The company took steps to prevent this happening again – fortunately, it was not a regular occurrence – but, still, its local image remained extremely poor. Matters became so bad that strikes were almost the rule rather than the exception, planning permission for vital extensions was refused and retention and recruitment of staff became impossible. Ostracized in the area, the company's survival seemed improbable.

So, it embarked upon a campaign to win over the locals. It provided a soccer pitch from spare land which it owned and, later, a pavilion and cricket pitch as well. It sponsored the local teams who, in turn, wore the company's logo on their strip.

It gave grants towards badly needed local initiatives in education and the health service, helping to provide libraries for school children and training facilities for the unemployed. It opened a crêche, mounted a huge leaflet campaign that explained the nature and importance of its chemicals and made sure that it fully retrained any employees who were threatened with redundancy before letting them go. It provided funds and work for the Youth Training Scheme and helped out as much as it could with the government's work in this area.

The result was a gradual and grudging shift in opinion. The company did not suddenly become 'Mr Clean' or experience a surge in popularity overnight. That would have been miraculous. But it did win respect for its intentions and its policy of putting its money where its mouth was.

It was undoubtedly an expensive community relations campaign but, faced with the problems of its circumstances, it saved the future of the plant.

Visiting speakers
Returning to the opportunities to contribute to locally-

based discussion, many organizations are open to visiting speakers. Women's Institutes, for instance, are often looking for speakers on a wide variety of subjects and their members are often influential in the community. A good speaker can be remembered for a long time, and the basic message that she or he gives lasts almost as long.

It follows that brushing up on your public speaking – or taking a course in it if you're not very confident – can be an important investment for your business.

Soon after the Austin Metro was launched, I gave a brief talk to the Soroptimists Club in Birmingham. The result was a better idea among the audience of professional business women and their spouses of the value to the West Midlands of a major local employer, a lasting impression of a determined management in BL which would not shirk tough decisions. The presentation also sold five Metros – although that had not been the object of the exercise.

In other words a twenty minute address resulted in a short-term return of several thousand pounds and a much more positive outlook on a company which had been widely perceived as a music hall joke.

Local clubs of all kinds – sporting, social and educational – are often grateful for interest in their activities expressed by an outsider. This is often repaid in time by increased business or, more likely, by increased co-operation when you next need it.

Adult education classes form another sector of public contact which is always on the lookout for facilities. Perhaps you have a meeting room or a canteen in which they can meet, or perhaps you could assist them in other ways. Even groups of ten to twenty people can be very influential in establishing your profile in the area.

Perhaps also you could loan a lorry to the local carnival procession; at the very least, it is an opportunity to show that you are supporting local charity. If you go the whole hog and organize the dressing of the float which the lorry carries, you may receive a generous amount of good publicity, especially if it wins the award for the Best Float.

This willingness to give time, equipment, goods or services free of charge to a local deserving cause or charity is usually highly productive in terms of a good name: A Peugeot dealer in our village holds garden fêtes, jumble sales, carol singing evenings and other events to raise money for the local hospital. It costs him nothing except the – considerable – time and effort he expends to organize and co-opt others. Its benefits to the hospital are considerable; its benefits to his business, equally so, although it would be wrong to imply that this is his motive. His reasons are very largely altruistic; nevertheless, our village, and areas all around, are swarming with Peugeots to a degree far beyond the cars' natural market share.

Local sponsorship
The next stage of development from this approach is the sponsoring of a local effort of some sort, usually in the arts or sports areas. A youth football team to whom you supply free kit will be quite willing to advertise your company by having your company name or logo prominently displayed on the jerseys. It may cost you a few hundred pounds (which you may be able to write off against tax), but you have positioned your company firmly in the local football community as well as having secured a strong identity for free advertising.

Your team might not make *Match of the Day* but it will impress the parents, teachers, friends and supporters who take an interest. Some of them may well be your own employees, others, potential customers, and the word of mouth recommendations your company will receive could be considerable.

That is an obvious example of a small start in the sponsorship world. The opportunities in any area are very considerable and require less expenditure than you might imagine. Often, recipients are happy to advertise and promote your product or services in return for product support only, without any money changing hands. If, for instance, you manufacture fencing panels and are willing to provide fencing for the local cricket field, tennis club or village hall, nobody is likely to object if you want to plaster your company name all over the finished product – provided it's tastefully done. That is something which is in your own interest anyway, as the fencing provides a highly visible example of your product and your marketing identity.

Carrying this example further, windbreaks are one of the latest trends in cost-effective, locally-based promotions. Those long, dark green canvas or plastic screens which surround tennis courts to keep out the worst of the swirling wind can be a very useful method of publicizing your company to a highly targeted audience.

Tennis courts are usually situated in private tennis clubs which boast a reasonable quota of wealthy members, who are, in turn, well connected in the local community. The windbreaks are erected at the beginning of the season in the Spring and remain up until about the end of September; indeed, some clubs leave them up all the year round.

You can buy windbreaks ready identified with your company name and logo for a matter of a few hundred pounds and they will have a life of at least five years. As well as being seen by the club members and players they often face outwards as well as inwards and can, therefore, be seen by all the passing traffic – a sort of up-market poster site for a fraction of the cost of the real thing.

If your product or service does not lend itself to this kind of application, then a straightforward cash donation is often the best way of attracting both gratitude and attention. Donations to charities are, of course, tax allowable within certain limits, so deserving causes to do with health or the environment are quite cost-effective methods of payment.

They don't have the publicity value of sponsoring a local event though, and for that reason you may wish to divide your largesse so that you do good in a number of different fields, thus also spreading the publicity net.

In the case of an event (such as a charity concert, garden fête, flower show, arts festival or sporting fixture) a donation will usually be acknowledged in the editorial copy of the programme and, perhaps, also on the publicity posters and leaflets. This is especially true if you become a 'Friend' or patron of the cause and this is all good grist to the mill in developing a positive profile for your company in the area and in selected circles.

There are also usually opportunities to display your own advertising or promotional material at the venue or nearby – perhaps in a small exhibition – and this is a facility which may not be accessible to ordinary advertisers.

Since local sponsorship is, by definition, small scale, your outlay in this area is unlikely to exceed the price of a good Christmas lunch for your staff. A tactically chosen and well followed through sponsorship programme will achieve considerable favourable attention, providing that it forms an integral part of a well thought out programme of local community relations.

Targeting influential circles

The keynote to this whole area of the community is to create a climate of goodwill in which to operate an efficient and successful business. It works on much the same principle as a storage heater: you pump in the heat when it is most advantageous to do so and call upon it when you need it.

So, list your problems and opportunities in the local area; list the people who have influence over the outcome of those issues and then discover what they do with themselves when they are not working and are not the object of your interest.

All local councillors, for instance, have some recreation or burning cause for which they are always in need of support.

Without descending to the level of corruption, a helping hand here and there can often be rewarded by a closer relationship with an influential councillor who happens to be, say, the Chairman of the Planning Committee with which you've been having so much trouble. If, during the course of a working lunch to discuss the issues of his or her pet interest, you happen to mention that you've been baulked several times by the Planning Committee – without whingeing about it – it is not beyond the bounds of possibility that the key councillors may look at the problem again from a fresh perspective – and who knows what will happen then.

I worked in local government in South Wales for two years and the decisions which were taken by most of the major committees – and, in particular, the Planning Committee – were undoubtedly influenced by seemingly irrelevant details. Once I became familiar with the complexities of small town politics, it became clear that many decisions were based on the perception of the applicant held by various councillors. Some applications were passed, not so much on merit as on who was requesting them. It was noticeable that businesses who had supported various local charities and other good causes were, almost invariably, looked upon with favour.

Large food retailers, with vested interests in developing out of town supermarkets, hypermarkets and shopping centres, spend a fortune on local community relations. They make presentations to every conceivable group of people who could influence the planning decision. They make provision in their proposals for new hospitals, schools or community centres and they often spend very considerable sums of money in the process. Unfortunately, they do not always buy the best, or the most discreet, advice and this – coupled with the popular image of property developers and estate agents – has tended to give the practice a dubious name.

Nevertheless, one of the strongest weapons in educating a local public is the co-ordinated campaign as practised by big developers. It includes the door-to-door delivery of hundreds of thousands of leaflets which set out the main issues in simple terms and present the developer's arguments in a compelling way.

This coincides with an exhibition – or series of exhibitions – usually held in the libraries and showing in graphic terms the environmental, social, economic and educational advantages of the proposed scheme.

A series of public meetings and debates is arranged at which the developer's representatives will meet anyone from the community who has a point of view and discuss the development in open forum. These can be quite lively events, sometimes just a bit too lively for the unfortunate representative....

Finally, there is the sugar on the pill: an announcement that the developer, or his client, will fund a new wing of the hospital, endow a chair at the university, build a new community centre free of charge or offer a number of scholarships to pupils in the area.

All this action can combine to form a pretty powerful argument in favour of a new development; even then, there are cases in which it might not work at the first time of asking. If, however, the dose is repeated often enough over a period of, say, ten years, the chances are that it will achieve its purpose.

So, community relations can cover a vast spectrum of activity, all designed to enable a commercial entity to grow in its chosen area with the minimum amount of interference and the maximum amount of support. Very often, the local community can benefit to a considerable degree from this attention and, in this case, one of those rare situations is created in which everybody wins.

One of the best ideas of recent times in the South East has been the willingness of commercial interests to plant a tree, copse or even a whole wood to replace trees lost in the great storm of October 1987. In a number of cases, the finished plantation has been named after the benefactor, thus leaving a lasting memorial to the thoroughness and vision of one who is adept in community relations.

There's a thought the next time you're digging the garden.

7   Sponsorship

We saw in the last chapter how sponsorship can be useful at a local level. At national and international levels the stakes, the rewards and the costs are very much higher. Consequently, many organizations who venture into the sponsorship game for the first time end up with burnt fingers, empty bank balances and precious little to show for it.

This is not to say that you shouldn't consider sponsorship, but it belongs to the second phase of your PR programme. It is not a pastime for the inexperienced and as a financial burden it can be colossal. As a key factor in increasing awareness, however, it can also have colossal impact.

The most widely sponsored activity is sport in various forms, ranging from the massive sums put into the Football League, professional golf or tennis to the sponsoring of a local, amateur team, individual player or event. A recently published survey showed that about 90 per cent of sponsorship money in the UK is spent on sport and, to give an indication of scale, this amounts to about £220 million.

The arts is the next most popular category, an area in which sponsorship has been encouraged by successive governments as a means of reducing the burden on the public purse while ensuring a reasonable level of continuing artistic activity. The emphasis here is traditionally placed on those forms of arts activities which are both physically and intellectually accessible to a general public, rather than being of interest only to an esoteric minority. This kind of activity is also, of course, more likely to be commercially rewarding.

Most of Britain's leading orchestras, for example, are sponsored to some degree, and very few musical tours of any form take place unless they are underwritten. Nevertheless, the popularity of the material is of prime importance, so, if you do feel like venturing into this heady world, sponsoring a tour by Madonna is more likely to prove successful than sponsoring a recital of all Scriabin's piano sonatas by an unknown music student.

A handful of minor activities clamour for attention and thinly spread cash, but the main arena is heavily sports based and it is there that most of the action occurs.

The benefits

What, then, are the benefits? Why do otherwise perfectly sane business people spend vast sums of hard-earned money on schemes which at times are harebrained, which would exercise the patience of a saint and for which, on paper at least, there appears to be very little return?

The answer is complex but includes the benefits of TV air time, the balance of the marketing mix, the association of brand with a strong visual image, an alternative outlet for legitimate marketing spend and, not least, the person's own interest in the sponsored activity.

Primarily, the lure of TV makes all the difference. The small screen commands vast audiences for many sporting occasions. The watching public can approach levels of over five million for such events as international football matches, the Wimbledon Tennis Tournament or the Olympic Games.

Sponsorship which carries TV coverage is, therefore, by far the easiest way to penetrate the mass market, much more visual than a daily newspaper and much more varied in its demographic audience profile than any of the national dailies which attain this kind of circulation.

If you're selling insurance, for instance, the *Star* is hardly the best market at which to aim; a cricket test match, played in front of TV audiences counted in the millions over a five-day period, gives a much wider marketing spread.

Thus, Cornhill Insurance placed a number of eggs in one basket by investing heavily in Test cricket for several years, so that all Tests played in England were officially called 'The Cornhill Insurance Test Match, England versus Australia – or whoever'. This identity had to be reproduced by all TV, radio and newspaper reporters covering the event as well as appearing on scoreboards, advertising and promotional literature.

It paid off, especially when the West Indies or Australia were visiting and the crowds, the excitement, the media attention and, therefore, the viewing figures were at a peak.

Most Olympic sponsorships are sold on the basis of the vast international TV coverage which the sponsors are supposed to receive. To a certain extent this is valid, although obscure sports broadcast in the middle of the night (formation swimming at 3.45 am, volleyball (Peru *v.* Roumania) at 5 am) do not often represent a highly successful sponsorship – especially for those who are putting up the money.

The impact on the game
Sponsorship also changes sport to a great degree. The professional tennis circuit has become a lot harder in many ways since commercial interests took over at the end of the 1960s. The circuit is unrelentingly gruelling, being fully international and played virtually all the year round with no respite or worthwhile close season. The matches often have to be scheduled to fit in with TV broadcast times (especially in the USA and Australia) and the prize money, having

reached telephone number dimensions, is out of all proportion to the activity.

Cricket, too, has never really settled down after the Kerry Packer World Cup circus of 1977 when coloured balls and pyjama-like clothes were used in evening matches played under floodlights for the first time to fit in to Channel 9 programme schedules.

The consequent improvement in players' rewards has not, some would say, affected any but the most internationally successful cricketers. Ian Botham and Viv Richards might earn a small fortune but there are still county players in England who are retained by their counties for less than £5,000 a year, hardly the security, let alone the riches, for which all the fuss was made over ten years ago.

And yet the standards of English Test cricket have dropped alarmingly over those ten years with defeats being regularly notched up against virtually every other cricketing country, partly because of the huge increase in limited over cricket encouraged by the Packer circus.

Golf and soccer are two more sports in which the ludicrously high level of reward owes much to TV-based sponsorships while even such sedentary occupations as snooker and darts have undergone a transformation for the small screen with sponsors injecting huge sums of money, largely for the benefit of the viewers in the sitting room.

One aspect of big time sports sponsorship of which to beware is the transient nature of TV's interest. For a sport such as snooker, the sudden propulsion from a largely amateur, localized pastime to the glaring national TV spotlight of *Pot Black* and its successors was a massive change. New stars emerged, were treated as national heroes – or villains – and were able to earn very large sums of money. But audience tastes are fickle and too much repetition breeds boredom. Viewing figures fell gradually but steadily over a period of, perhaps, six or seven years and, when audience figures fall, the interest of TV editors and sponsors alike wanes in sympathy.

Thus, snooker is now televised much less frequently and the sport may well become better for it by finding its natural level once again. The sponsors, notably Embassy cigarettes, had achieved their objective of wide awareness and were ready to switch attention to new fields.

The marketing mix

The second reason for sponsorship, and conceptually the most valid, is that it represents an integral part of the marketing mix in a sensibly run company. Vast sums are spent – and some are wasted – each year on advertising above the line. Considerable sums are spent on promotional activities of other kinds, such as direct mail, point of sale, exhibitions and sponsorship. In this mix, sponsorship is as valuable – occasionally more so if mass brand awareness is the objective – than any other element. But it is not, in isolation, the answer to a company's identity problems any more than any one of the other factors might be.

Visibility at events or the knowledge that your company sponsors an individual or a team effort can greatly enhance your company's profile and help to make it a recognizable name across a wide variety of spheres. But what it can't do is persuade a watching public that you're any better than your competition or that you offer particularly good value for money. It is, therefore, a device to increase public recognition and awareness, but it is not a device which will necessarily increase appreciation of your company.

Brand associations

The third reason is an extension of this point, the association of brand values. That is, the way in which the viewing public links the sponsoring brand with the activity or sportsperson in the limelight. Sometimes this link may be subconscious and the image is retained in the mind quite subliminally. If you watch Viv Richards crash a boundary, the retained image is usually frozen at the point at which the ball comes off the bat – helped in the last few years by TV techniques such as slow motion replays and freeze frame. At this critical point in the memory's retention the brand name on the bat is highly visible and makes a forceful impact.

On a more specific note, this association is often to be found in the way in which companies linked to particular activities provide free equipment to leading individuals in their chosen world.

Viv Richards uses a Slazenger bat and the association of his power, elegance and success with the Slazenger brand name is self-explanatory. Likewise, John McEnroe and Steffi Graf use a Dunlop tennis racket with which to sweep aside their opponents. Theirs is a quality which many aspiring club tennis players would like to emulate and, therefore, they choose an identical racket. The prowess might be different but the equipment at least is the same.

In fact, McEnroe must rank as one of the most successful sponsorships of all time, not because he won so often or because he played with speed and skill but because he was seldom out of the news – for one reason or another – and therefore gave excellent value to the brand he endorsed.

However, players of his calibre are not so hard up that they have to beg a free tennis racket. On the contrary, they can – and do – pick and choose the manufacturer, the product and the brand with which they wish to be associated. Consequently, tennis racket manufacturers – and other sports firms – spend huge sums of money trying to entice the top players to use or 'endorse' their equipment in an ever increasing spiral of bidding which threatens to turn the game topsy-turvy.

In 1985, Dunlop Slazenger signed a new contract with McEnroe for three years and agreed to pay a six figure retainer in each of those three years. If this is added to his other sponsorship deals, McEnroe 'earned' over $2.5 million a year just for walking on court properly dressed and equipped. He was also obliged to dedicate a small number of days each year to promotional activities for his sponsors, but the time for each sponsor amounted to less than a week and his activities were strictly limited to posing for photos, interviewing and appearing at events in a non-playing role.

Of course not all sponsorships are in this league of international limelight, but an increasing number are. So, if you want to start making your mark at that kind of level, you have to have a substantial sum of money with which to play.

Brand values can also cross-fertilize to a greater extent than always meets the eye. If you run a company which provides a worthy but unexciting product or service, sponsoring an activity which is exciting or glamorous can imbue your own product with some of those qualities in the eyes of the customers.

If, for instance, you are in something as dull as the life assurance business, with a low public visibility and an even lower level of understanding, a tangible expression of your existence can be made through the sponsorship of a major event in the arts world.

This is partly why Standard Life sponsored a production of a new Bernstein opera on its UK tour. This is also why Barclays Bank spent a fortune on sponsoring the Football League. It did not need the awareness in itself, it *did* need the awareness to be associated with something tough, competitive and highly visible to a mass market.

Similarly, a number of non-motoring companies like to sponsor various forms of motor sport in the hope that a Formula One racing car hurtling round a circuit will remind us all of Digital Computers or Benetton fashions. The association of style, excitement and glamour as well as performance and achievement makes this kind of sponsorship particularly attractive which, given the immense costs of Grand Prix racing, is just as well – for the sport.

Durex is happy to sponsor the Suzuki Motor Cycle Racing Team as a complementary image which embodies speed, safety, quality, high levels of skill and the ability to handle power responsibly as well as macho appeal – exactly the kind of audience at which the product is aimed.

Increasingly, too, companies are putting money into sponsorship because they can no longer put it into other marketing activities such as advertising. This is particularly true of the tobacco companies who are now not allowed to advertise in certain areas; it is also true, although to a lesser extent, of the drinks companies.

As social conscience increases, it seems likely that this trend will be extended to other areas of business and that we shall see larger sponsorships from a broad cross section of business which, for various reasons is unwilling or unable to sustain a worthwhile spend in advertising terms. Even now, companies like Rothmans and Marlboro are giants in the sponsorship world and their chosen sponsorships are often closely associated with sporting, healthy, outdoor activities.

In the same way, the Ford Motor Company is sufficiently concerned with the environment and the impact of carbon monoxide fumes on the atmosphere that it sponsors a European-wide Environmental Award Scheme which fixes Ford's social and environmental responsibility firmly in the minds of those who are involved and, to a lesser extent, in the minds of those who read about it. It could, of course, simply advertise the fact that most of its vehicles can now run on unleaded fuel and are socially responsible (some advertising is already devoted to this aspect) but the Environmental Awards are a much more effective way of getting across the message of social and environmental responsibility to those who are in the forefront of the Green and related movements because they are the people with whom Ford actually works in this exercise. It's the sort of sponsorship which most of the other motor manufacturers wish they had thought of first.

Staying with social responsibility, a massive change is already underway – not just in sponsorship, but in the whole approach to marketing. That is the movement away from sex. Ever since the cool model proclaimed that 'Nigel says Polish bacon is the best' adverts of 1964 and the Manikin cigar girls rolled at the edge of the surf on a sun-drenched beach a few years later, sex has been overtly or implicitly behind a great deal of marketing, especially advertising. Even the term 'sexy' in marketing parlance means attractive in a marketing, commercial or sales sense not in a conventionally sexual sense. The advent of AIDS – and, perhaps, public boredom – are combining to change that. Whatever qualities we will be selling in ten years' time, they will not include sex.

Finally, there is often an element of personal interest or involvement with the chosen activity. Most company chairmen have sports, arts or other activities in which they have a special interest; if they don't, their spouses invariably do, and the result is often a dislocated sponsorship which bears no obvious relationship to the business of the company concerned.

This is all right if there is a requirement to lose the odd £50,000 for tax purposes. If money is tight, however, it can often be an irritant for the Marketing Director who is trying to focus the marketing activities towards related fields – and more than an irritant to the Finance Director who is trying to achieve a profit.

Clearly, this approach is unprofessional and usually counterproductive to the business concerned, but there can be exceptions: when the hunch works brilliantly or when the company's end product matches and complements the activity involved, perhaps more by good luck than judgement.

The approach

So, these tend to be the main reasons why businesses invest huge sums of money in sponsorships; but what areas should you examine for sponsorship opportunities and what should you look out for if you decide to go ahead?

First, try to ensure that there is a relevance to your business in the activity – and the image of that activity – that you are going to sponsor. Unless there is a connection that is either obvious or can be made so, it is likely that you will be pouring considerable sums of money down the drain.

In deciding this, approach it from the same point of view as most publicity and marketing programmes: decide what you want out of the deal before you even begin talking to people.

Do you want greater awareness of your business? If so, in what demographic sectors? Do you want to appeal directly to existing and potential customers or indirectly to those who influence them? Do you want the sponsorship to provide you with an entertainment forum for valued customers or employees as well as, or instead of, possible sales leads? How much do you want to spend – not just as a finite sum but as a percentage of your overall marketing spend? Have you left enough budget to capitalize on the sponsorship? If your team wins, you may want to run advertisements telling everyone that you have sponsored a winning side, thus sharing publicly in their success. If you're sponsoring an arts activity, you want as many people as possible to know about your involvement and that is seldom done, or achieved by any arts body. Who is going to control the sponsorship from your company to ensure that you get full value?

Work from these premises backwards so that you can arrive at a marketing-led decision rather than one which is based on instinct or personal interest. This way, you're more likely to hit the right combination of circumstances to enhance your company image.

For example, if broad awareness is your aim, the first stage is to research the areas in which you need that awareness: the market sectors in which you sell or hope to sell. If these are national, then you may need a national sponsorship, possibly even an international one if you're focusing on export markets. But, don't be tempted to be too ambitious; sponsorship costs far more than merely the sum of money that you pay to the event or organization that you're sponsoring.

Does the activity to be sponsored reflect the kind of image which you want your company, your service or your product to project? If it doesn't the chances are that the sponsorship will not be very successful because nobody will be able to see the logic of your decision or to voluntarily make the link between the two entities. So make sure that there is, at the very least, compatibility between the two and, preferably, an obvious connection.

This way the qualities which you are selling are reflected in the activities you are sponsoring. So, if you manufacture and sell toothpaste, there might not be a great deal of point in sponsoring the National Windsurfing Championships; better to try a concert tour by George Michael. If you run a chain of estate agents, there's probably not a lot of mileage in sponsoring a fashion show; try a Young Architects' competition instead.

Sponsorships do not, of course, have to be bought off the peg as a ready-made package, although they usually are. If you have the time, the resource, the money and the bright idea to create an event or promotion of your own, then you may find that it works better then anything you could buy – at least it will be exclusive, and that's a great thing in sponsorship. But, be careful. If it's that good an idea, why hasn't somebody else already thought of it and put it into practice? It may be that they've discovered that it's unworkable or too expensive or both.

Do you want to appeal directly to a target audience of customers and potential customers or do you want to appeal to the influencers on their lives? For example, if you manufacture bicycles, it may pay to sponsor the police to tour schools with a road safety presentation which you have created and, subtly, branded by loaning bicycles and other equipment. This will appeal to the children who may want a bike but who are not going to buy one. By going a stage further and providing a leave-behind hand-out document, you can reach their parents and teachers in an ostensibly uncommercial way, but in a way which is even more persuasive than the most blatant advertising.

Then, look very carefully at the package you are being offered before you sign anything. Most major sponsorships are handled by a promotions or sponsorship consultancy. (These are a sort of brokers who will undertake to attract sponsors for an event or activity in exchange for a fairly hefty fee.) Be careful. Most of these companies are perfectly respectable but others are opportunists who don't much care what you get out of it provided they get their money. It is an area of marketing which has attracted more than its fair share of rogues. Moreover, the very significant growth rate which is still being sustained across sponsorship activities suggests that there will be no shortage of bright young entrants eager to make a quick buck.

Above all, don't forget that you are not the client. The consultancy will treat you as a customer to whom they will sell as much as they can for as much money as they can. Sometimes, a consultancy will offer a 'full service package' to ensure that you receive full value out of your sponsorship. This is another area where they make their money by offering a PR and publicity service on your behalf to maximize your media coverage and arrange all the various promotional activities which are so necessary. Often, the consultancy will simply not be equipped to do this professionally. When one is, beware that you're not opening up your company to another PR consultancy, who, by nature of the contract on which it is working, is more interested in the short-term return than a long standing improvement in your image. Their charges for these services will also be additional to the original sponsorship cost which you've agreed and, since they are primarily a sponsorship company, they may not be all that brilliant at PR – or any other marketing activities.

It would be foolish to suggest that all sponsorship consultancies are like this. Some offer excellent value for money and do a professional and honest job but few are in this league.

Another important precaution is to make sure that you check out all the small print in the contract. Look, for example, at the amount of guaranteed media coverage. Many sponsorship companies merrily float out phrases like 'twenty hours of prime TV airtime' which is fine until you realize it applies only to broadcasts to the Outer Hebrides at 3 am or, more commonly, that they are basing this claim on a vague discussion with someone at a TV station who has no authority to even hazard a guess at what coverage may be planned. You must have a guarantee in writing that is worth the paper it's written on, otherwise you can waste a great deal of money and end up being very disappointed.

Beware also the glib promoter who assures you that 'while nobody can guarantee telly, we're working on it at the moment and it's only a question of time before they come to the party.' Fine; let them come to the party before you do. Then you'll know who your fellow guests will be.

Once the TV chiefs have agreed in writing to give a reasonable amount of coverage, then is the time for you to accept your invitation and not before. Sometimes in this situation, a sponsorship consultancy might try to increase the asking price because of TV commitment. Have nothing to do with this. The sponsorship was originally offered to you including substantial, if unspecified, air time. All that has happened since is that a programme editor has sorted out his schedule and final broadcast slots. That is no reason why the sponsorship consultancy should rake in another few thousand pounds from your hard-earned budget.

Beware, too, the restrictions placed on advertising in the event. If you've agreed to sponsor, say, a soccer team, you want to make sure that your name appears clearly on the team's shirts at all games – especially those which are televised. It's no good spending all that money to discover that the TV channel's policy is not to broadcast matches involving teams with sponsored or branded strips.

Likewise, check the legality, siting and visibility of advertising hoardings around the ground. They will, no doubt, be seen by a few thousand faithful each week, but you want them to be seen by a few million unfaithful at least once or twice a season.

Programme 'mentions' (literally, the number of times your company name appears in the printed programme of the sponsored event) can be another source of contention. Petty though it sounds, it is worth insisting on not only the number of mentions but also the size, position, frequency and colour. Otherwise, you may find that you've been unfortunately overlooked by a 'printer's error' and you've no legal redress. An example of this which can be particularly irritating is a mention of your company which ignores your logo and corporate identity – even though you'd lavished money on them – and simply sticks down your name in any old typeface which happens to be at hand.

Once you've embarked upon your sponsorship and devised the strategy by which you are going to maximize its value, you need someone to run it on your behalf. The sponsorship consultancy will do this and so will your normal PR consultancy – if you've got one – but they'll both want a special fee for the privilege. Your advertising agency probably won't touch it even with a special fee.

In any case, nobody external is ever really going to have the same motivation in furthering and protecting your interest as an in-house employee. So it's well worth detailing somebody from your Marketing Department who is enthusiastic and professional and whom you can trust to represent your interests conscientiously. He or she then assumes total responsibility for the success of the sponsorship (a useful project in a career development context, incidentally) and focuses all the strategically planned activity into one office.

The bottom line

From all this it can be seen that you are going to have to spend a great deal more money in maximizing your sponsorship than might have been apparent at first. Indeed, the general rule of thumb is to double the amount that you are paying in direct sponsorship fees.

This clearly puts the whole exercise in a different light. If you have the odd £50,000 kicking about that you wouldn't miss too much – that's one thing. But when you think about allocating another £50,000 to doing the job properly and making sure that the first £50,000 isn't wasted – that's something else again.

You have to tell people that you're doing this sponsorship – otherwise there's no point in doing it – and that in itself costs money. You will need:

1 An advertising allocation over and above what you would normally spend.
2 A specially dedicated PR allocation to maximize the reporting of your angle – because nobody else will do that for you.
3 A whacking great entertainment budget for all the guests you are hosting – and you're usually stuck with caterers of somebody else's choosing and pricing.
4 Travel and subsistence costs – which can be high because everybody regards it as a jolly.

5 A promotional budget for all the T-shirts, hats, banners, posters, stickers, labels, brochures, balloons and bits and pieces without which, somehow, the whole exercise seems irrelevant.

Above all, you need the time and resources to make sure that your own company's interests are being vigorously promoted along with, or in excess of, everybody else's. Without this element, the whole thing is futile.

So, start with something modest and budget for the worst. Your local football team, perhaps, or any of the sports teams, clubs and activities which fit your customer profile: squash, rugby, tennis, athletics, fencing, badminton, horse riding events. All appeal to different market sectors and most are relatively low cost activities with a need, and an appreciation, for funding.

If the arts have particular relevance, or fit your target market more exactly, look at local repertory productions, music festivals, concerts, amateur art exhibitions, school painting competitions, youth orchestras and ensembles and soloists.

Otherwise, there are opportunities to sponsor career development in many professions and skills: 'Young Engineer competitions' (which often attract considerable media coverage) and various ways of supporting local education and youth groups. You might have an old portacabin which could become a new Scout hut or an old crewbus which could become a new school minibus.

Do not be tempted to be too ambitious too soon. Evaluate the return of your early sponsorship activities very closely before branching out or committing further money. Often, the value lies in the impact of sponsoring an event or activity for the first time and this impact can wane as the relationship continues. As with snooker on TV, it ceases to be novel and becomes jaded, or the audience falls away until the target market is no longer strongly represented.

This is the time to call a halt and cast round for other sponsorship outlets, or time to count the cost, assess the return and take a decision on the principle of entering into a new sponsorship package. In some cases, it may not be worth it.

All in all, therefore, sponsorship is not a venture to be undertaken lightly.

But it does have its uses, especially if you employ it on a relatively small, local scale as an exercise in extending the goodwill which your company commands in the area. And it is useful for both external and internal audiences. Many of your employees may be interested in attending a performance, match or other event – indeed, some organizers will arrange special previews for sponsors' employees – and this is a good way of improving morale in a different and imaginative way.

But, the golden rule is to remember that, despite all the fine words and the glowing promises, nobody ever really looks after the interests of the sponsor except that sponsor.

8   Internal communications

I once met a man in Walsall who was organizing a seminar on Employee Communications for one of the professional management bodies. Fortunately, I can't remember which one. As we were discussing the position of the podium, or some other burning issue, he said, 'You know, I don't believe in all this communicating nonsense. The only thing my workers understand is a big boot up the backside. All this talking to them is a load of poppycock.'

He didn't really say either 'backside' or 'poppycock' but I'm sure you've grasped the gist of his argument. He was probably the most atavistic manager I've ever met; he didn't really agree with votes for women, either. And he was running a small company, one in which it should have been a simple matter to communicate properly.

The hardest audience of all
Yet, his attitude is still all too common especially in some of the more traditional industries such as engineering and slavery. And the attitude is prevalent throughout companies of all sizes. Consequently these are the very climates in which strikes and other industrial relations difficulties are most likely to happen.

Do you remember what it was like when you first started work? Did anyone ever tell you as much as you needed or wanted to know? Do you now tell your employees everything they need to know? Do you tell them what you expect of them?

Nobody actually wants to go on strike – except perhaps committed Trotskyists and they're pretty rare. People only strike because they're allowed to in much the same way that schoolchildren only misbehave because they can get away with it. Strikes are almost always a sign of weak or inept management rather than strong or heavily principled trade unionism.

Strikes are also usually a sign of fear or deep-seated insecurity. There may be a rumour that jobs are at risk or that working practices are to be drastically updated. There may be a feeling among the employees that the company isn't doing very well and that security is threatened. It is amid this kind of rumour and uncertainty that militancy thrives. And it is exactly this kind of rumour and uncertainty that good communications can prevent.

A workforce who know roughly what is going on within their company are more likely to have confidence in it, themselves and their future. Consequently, they're much less likely to do something daft. They realize what they've got to lose. They are also likely to be prepared to work harder and more conscientiously which usually results in higher and more consistent levels of quality in what they are doing.

So how do you go about gaining and retaining their confidence and trust? How do you win over their hearts and minds?

You communicate with them.

It's not easy; in any organization your own employees are your hardest audience. But they're also your most important. They are the ones you need most. They are the ones who can make or break your business almost at will and this applies equally to giant multinationals and to two-man bands. So, you've got to treat them as the colleagues they are and communicate with them fully and openly. Otherwise, they'll never build trust and confidence in you. And if you can't rely on your employees, you'd be better off closing the book here and going to farm sheep in the Welsh hills. Sheep don't answer back.

The honest approach

Talking to your employees is a bit like talking to your parents: most people find they have a mental block about it until it's too late. Perhaps this is partly because what is needed in both cases is the ability to be ruthlessly honest, not just with your audience but, in the process, with yourself.

But, like most problems, the best way to deal with this is to face up to it and make the effort. Once that barrier has been breached, it's very much easier. When you've got into the habit of communicating regularly with those you employ, you'll be surprised at the way in which the process can develop into a two-way dialogue and you can find out more about your company and the people who work in it than you ever dreamed went on.

Of course, this has its drawbacks. You may not actually want to know who's secretly going out with whom, let alone what some of the staff were saying about you at the last Christmas party, but that's all part of the fun of running your business.

There are two approaches in talking to your employees: you can tell them what they don't need or want to know (this is quite common) or you can be professional about it and go about the exercise in a more honest and constructive way.

Although most of the examples in this chapter are drawn from a large company concerned with avoiding industrial relations difficulties and improving a generally low morale, they are equally valid for any size of company or other organization which employs even a handful of people at any level. And they will serve to focus on some of the core principles upon which effective communication is based.

What they don't want is to be given:

- *Promises you can't keep* – new BMWs for all the staff next year.
- *Conflicting messages* that do not tally with your public statements. Employees quickly sense any inconsistencies between statements for internal and external use. You may, and should, re-phrase or re-emphasize a document for internal use but it must contain essentially the same message as your public statements.
- *Jam tomorrow* – a new bonus scheme will be introduced once we're achieving 50 per cent profit; they don't know what 50 per cent profit is, let alone how unlikely it is.
- *Sales hype* – 'This is the best product on the market today, ladies and gentlemen, with added value, super secret ingredient AVF47/pty6 and our unique three week guarantee.' Come off it; your employees make or work with this wonder product – there's not much they don't know about it.
- *The marketing approach* – similar to the sales hype but laced with all sorts of meaningless clichés like 'share of voice', 'shifting the tin' (widely used by car companies), single minded propositions, anytime foods, fighting for shelf space, demographic breakdowns...you know the rest.
- *Patronizing talk* – 'Now none of you need to worry about details like financial results or takeover bids – you just keep on being the salt of the earth.'
- *Management jargon that goes over their heads* – 'The current situation is the inevitable outcome of historical undercapitalization juxtaposed with overreaching diversification.' In other words, you're bust. So say so.

Nor do employees want to be talked to too often or, worse still, not often enough. In all, it's a very delicate balance and frequency of communication is a topic to which we'll return later in the chapter.

What employees do want is, fortunately, easier both to describe and to carry out.

- Quite simply, *it's the truth*.
- The truth about the business which pays their wages and salaries.
- What its prospects are.
- A clear indication of where it's been, where it is now and where it's going to.
- Above all, they want to know what role they themselves can and must play in its future.

It's good to feel wanted and that's what a great deal of positive employee communications is all about: reassurance that they have a future – and a useful one – as your employees. It's not really much to ask, but it's amazing how few managers ever say it.

Providing that the truth – or enough of it – is honestly presented in a straightforward way, your store with even the hardest employee will steadily rise. On top of this, the giving and receiving of information becomes a habit and, before very long, you'll begin to find your employees expecting you to communicate with them. They may even run a sweepstake on the content or length of your presentation – just as though they were preparing for a sermon in Church.

And the more they expect regular communication, the more they'll listen and come to regard it for what it is: a fundamental part of your job and a basic management right. And, seen in that context of a necessary part of managing the business and its people, the act of communicating will increase the respect in which you are held.

Fine. That should render some of the Personnel Department redundant with a consequent saving on all those luncheon vouchers and Maestro HLEs. But exactly how do you go about this whole process?

How do you communicate with a workforce and especially with a workforce which doesn't seem to be particularly keen on listening? There are, again, two major routes, but this time, they both have a valuable role to play. There's the _written word_ and there's the _spoken word_.

The written word

Traditionally, the written word has been that good old warhorse: the Company Newspaper. There's a time honoured pattern to the Company Newspaper. It usually has a statement from the Chairman on the front page, a pretty girl, reasonably well clad, on page three, a centre spread of the girls on the switchboard on their Away Day to Brighton, a classified ad section (free), a births, marriages, deaths and divorces section, a crossword, a cookery column, a holiday competition, an angling column, a What's-On-in-Bognor section and, finally, a couple of pages devoted to in-jokes about the works soccer, cricket, squash, hockey and lacrosse teams.

And it's a time honoured profession, too. There are annual awards for the best company newspapers. There's even a sort of trade union for those who have the unenviable task of putting the things together: the British Association of Industrial Editors. As an institution, the Company Newspaper has even been immortalized by Reggie Perrin, and there are few higher accolades than that.

It seems a pity, then, that the whole concept is roughly fifty years out of date.

I used to edit the _Austin Morris Express,_ a monthly which went to about 50,000 employees, contained all the sort of things a paper like this should contain and was very highly regarded by those who believe in company newspapers.

One day, when I'd noticed great piles of the things lying virginally on the factory floor, I instigated a survey to find out what people thought about it. The results were depressing.

The main problem was that it was seen to be propagandist, worthy, intrusive, irrelevant, lightweight, highbrow, Birmingham-based (to employees in Oxford), Oxford-based (to people in Birmingham), London-based (to people in both Birmingham and Oxford – unique solidarity here) and, anyway, they all took the *Sun* or the *Financial Times*.

The difficulty is that it's impossible to pretend to be both a social paper and a business paper. So the answer is, not to try.

Your responsibility is to tell your employees about the business that pays their mortgages and rents. So tell them about it. In a business document. If they're crazy about the sports and social side of life, give them an annual grant towards a Sports and Social Club and let them get on with it.

The two-tier approach
In terms of formal communication (that is, the official business and routine communications, not the informal and impromptu chats in the canteen) to have one briefing document for all levels of staff would be a bit like making the entire population of the UK read the *Daily Express*. And that would ultimately satisfy nobody. There is, therefore, merit in creating a briefing document for what can loosely be termed management and a performance bulletin for what are tactfully known as 'hourly paid' employees.

The *management briefing* is usually issued weekly or fortnightly – even daily in very fast changing businesses like the music industry. It contains a summary of points about the business which management find helpful: production, sales, quality, reject rates, financial performance, possible problems of supply, advance warning of disruption or changes or even big orders. Industrial relations matters are often referred to as well and, if space permits, a short section on the overall industrial or commercial sector in which the company operates can share the corporate intelligence with those who most need to know it. Sometimes Board decisions are recorded but that is usually best left to a specialized communications process involving the directors personally briefing their senior managers.

Production is cheap and cheerful; there's no need for it to be anything other than a well typed and laid out photocopy spread across perhaps four A5 pages. With the increasingly widespread use of desktop publishing on microcomputers, there are more imaginative designs and methods which still only cost a few pounds.

Distribution should be as regular as clockwork so that management get into the habit of expecting it and relying upon it for a source of information. Within weeks, they are likely to be complaining if it arrives ten minutes late. That's when you know it's performing its function properly.

The *performance bulletin* for employees is a trickier document to write, partly because this level of the workforce don't need – or want – so much information in such detail. Neither do they want to see a glossy publication which has obviously had money spent on it. That money could be more usefully deployed in their pay packets – another powerful argument against the company newspaper.

The information must be short, simple and to the point. In a manufacturing operation, for example, the key topics are reports on production achievement, quality levels, bonus awards (the bit everyone looks at first, like the last page of a thriller) cost levels (but only those about which the employees concerned can do something, otherwise it will only serve to infuriate), sales performance, running changes in production schedules or working practices and, perhaps, the installation of new plant and other more general information.

It's also a good idea if space is left to constantly hammer away at the various regular messages in the fields of safety at work and good housekeeping. No matter how much nagging employees get about these topics, there's always room for more.

If this bulletin is distributed via the foremen or supervisors, it also reinforces their authority as the bringers of news and information and, at the same time, provides them with the opportunity to review with their team the performance and priorities which govern their work. It becomes, in fact, the lifeline of the company's communications.

The oral approach

The written approach, although useful and necessary, is only part of the overall process and pieces of paper can have their drawbacks. Documents handed to employees are reassuring to the recipient in that they imply your commitment to what is contained in them. They have recorded for posterity your views on certain issues and, more importantly to the recipient, your commitment to something concrete or the true position of your enterprise.

This can be a double-edged sword. It can lead to employees expecting something mentioned in a bulletin written seven years ago and then promptly forgotten by everybody else. It can, in extreme cases, be used as evidence at industrial tribunals or in courts of law. Nobody can accurately predict exactly what will happen to their companies over a sustained period of time and, with no intent to mislead, information can become obsolete or irrelevant. But this may not be understood by all concerned. There may, for instance, be changes of management or other factors which blow good intentions off course.

Above all, the written word does not allow any two-way dialogue. Employees very seldom take up the optimistic offers of company newspaper editors that usually go along the despairing lines of 'This is *your* newspaper. We want to hear *your* views on ...' partly because the written word is not the natural medium of expression of many employees and also because the topics about which they feel strongly may not be raised in such a document, thus making it less than easy to broach a new and, perhaps, sensitive issue.

To create a genuine dialogue – often the only real way of gauging the mood of the workforce and of allowing steam to be let off in a relatively harmless way, you must talk to them direct and, what's even more important, let them talk to you direct in return. Only by doing so can they really feel that you listen to and care about their point of view, that you realize that they have feelings and that part of your job of managing the company is to listen, reassure and encourage.

In the autumn of 1979, for example, British Leyland stood at a nadir in its history. It was a music hall joke with a reputation for unreliable cars and permanently striking workers. The customers were deserting in droves, the dealers were defecting to other marques, the politicians were crying for an end to the massive public funding which was all that was keeping BL alive and industrial relations were at an all time low.

In the midst of all this a Streamlining Plan was announced by the then Chairman, Sir Michael Edwardes. It called for the closure of thirteen factories and the redundancy of over 10,000 employees on top of the large number which had already left.

The militant union convener at Longbridge, Derek Robinson, better known to the tabloid press as 'Red Robbo', immediately mounted a bid to defeat this plan and, in the process this management, by launching an alternative plan which safeguarded jobs by means of further massive public investment. The company offered to put the matter to an employee ballot – at that time almost unheard of in British industry.

The stage was thus set for one of the biggest and most radical industrial communications exercises of recent times. This was an occasion when the hearts and minds of all the employees had to be won over in a few short weeks and no amount of paper floating about the place could hope to do that.

The solution proved to be a personal tour of all the volume car plants – the largest part of the company – by the Austin Morris Managing Director, Harold Musgrove. His task was simple: to show the employees what they should have been shown years before, the future of the company. He graphically illustrated this by revealing the new cars they would be making (both on slide and in the flesh), the investment in plant and technology for the Metro (not then launched and the subject of a massive £280 million development programme) and, above all, the role which the shop floor employees themselves had to play in the company's future. Harold did not directly address either the Streamlining Plan or the ballot, although he expressed his personal opinion if he was asked for it.

The organizational task was formidable. At that time Austin Morris consisted of over 40,000 employees spread across seven factories throughout England, most operating night and day shifts. We created a thirty minute presentation outlining the current state of the company, the plans we had to tackle it, the new models upon which those plans were based, the investment in the factories and the likely job security of the foreseeable future.

When he'd presented all that, Harold embarked upon the hardest job of all: he threw the meeting open to the floor and took any questions the audiences cared to ask him – that was the most ambitious and the most successful part of the whole scheme. No attempt was made to discredit either the unions or Derek Robinson; instead, the union representatives at each plant were dutifully invited to the presentation, although few turned up.

The logistics were horrendous, even by the standards of a company which seldom slept. The 40,000 employees were covered in thirty-seven presentations held over a period of seven continuous working days and nights. No audience numbered more than 1200 and each plant received its own personalized presentation which had to be created after the previous one finished – often overnight.

This invariably involved new slides and other material and the M1 was kept very busy with cars ferrying scripts, slides and videos up and down.

To make matters worse, the Plan clearly spelled the end of the much respected MG plant at Abingdon and this did not guarantee a warm reception anywhere, either inside or outside the company.

The overall result however was well worth the very considerable effort and investment. The ballot resulted in an 86 per cent vote in favour of the company's Streamlining Plan and the days of the militant supremacy within BL were numbered from that moment.

One incident sticks out in my mind. It was the reaction of the notoriously militant night shift at Drews Lane – a singularly unglamorous part of Birmingham. To a man they stood and cheered at the end of the presentation. Unlike some other plants there were no awkward questions – just relief that they were to have some sort of future which, difficult and fraught though it might have been painted, was at least an end to the uncertainty of years and some sort of hope for a continuing job.

Afterwards I asked an elderly worker why there had been such an overwhelming response. 'Why,' he said. 'I've worked in this plant for twenty-eight years and that's the first time I've even *seen* a Managing Director, let alone had one come down on to the shop floor to talk to me. And what's more, he was prepared to listen to *us*. It's bloody fantastic.'

Without that marathon road show, it is unlikely that the Streamlining Plan would have been approved. Had it been thrown out, the BL board was honour bound to go back to the Department of Industry and report that, in their opinion, there was no alternative but to place the entire BL corporation in the hands of the receiver. That would probably have involved the loss of about 100,000 jobs and the entire British owned-volume car industry.

Since then the concept has been adopted with variations such as video through many areas of British industry. For office staff or shop-floor employee, there is no substitute for the eyeball to eyeball presentation.

Communicating through managers

Very few managers, even in today's relatively enlightened atmosphere, are trained properly in the art of communicating. Public speaking courses, for instance, are not yet part and parcel of a manager's education in the same way that, say, budgetary control or basic personnel or computing skills are.

Yet, without the ability to communicate, the responsibility to do so cannot fairly be vested in a manager. Without this responsibility, managers are not fulfilling their role. Moreover, any manager's morale is rapidly going to suffer if he or she feels that a fundamental part of the job is beyond them.

There are two answers to this problem. The first is, not surprisingly, to train managers in the basics of communicating with their employees. This should cover presentation and public speaking training, elementary behavioural psychology and assertiveness training, organizing and chairing group meetings, creating trust, writing bulletins, building relationships and marketing concepts to the workforce.

Once this level of expertise has been gained, the manager's job description can, and must, include specific responsibility to establish and sustain communications with those employees in his or her charge. Moreover, at periodic reviews, managers must be assessed on achievement in this area in the same way as they are assessed on the ability to work within budgets.

The second answer, which does not replace the first but reassures managers in the short term, is to provide them with the ammunition to fire the shots. One example found in most companies is the Annual Results.

A Works Manager is not necessarily familiar with much of the financial terminology himself, yet he is expected to explain the results – and, what's worse, their significance – to the employees. Most stand up in front of all their employees to give a demonstration of how to get stage fright, brain fade and tongue tied all at once.

If, as is increasingly the case, that Manager has a set of slides, an easy to follow script and a background briefing of the salient points on the Results, his credibility can be enhanced rather than eroded and the employees can receive genuine clarification and reassurance that they are working for a professional organization which is actively supporting its management.

These packages can vary depending on the requirement, but the most effective are the most simple because they are the most appealing and understandable. They also tend to be the least expensive.

The indirect approach

So far we have looked at ways in which to address your employees directly and in most cases this will be the most appropriate form of action.

However, there can be times when it is desirable that you communicate to your employees through a third party such as the press. During an industrial dispute for example when feelings are running high it is all too easy to have direct communication dismissed as propaganda and this may tarnish the credibility of your normal communication for some considerable time afterwards.

There is also a belief that the press and media are generally objective in their views, presenting impartial third party comment and that if something is in the paper, it is probably true. If it is not true then at least it is less prone to bias than a management document.

So in times of extreme need, do not be afraid to harness the media to your cause. However, do be careful that this does not become blatant, otherwise the journalist will feel exploited and cease to be helpful or even become actively unhelpful. Influencing the workforce through the media at times of necessity, therefore, must be approached with subtlety. On the basis that it is much easier to get negative stories into the press than positive ones, obtaining the volume of coverage can be too easy. British Leyland, for instance, used to – and may still – employ people to keep the company's troubles out of the papers rather than the more usual PR role of trying to gain coverage.

Also, local papers and radio stations usually have contacts inside factories and offices and with union officials. Sometimes they pay employees to inform them of any juicy titbits of news. Consequently, they are often better and earlier informed than you are and this calls for special caution. Be careful not only in your public statements but also in all your internal utterances for, in the words of the cliché, 'Today's Clock Notice is Tomorrow's Headline' and this is never more true than at times of industrial dispute.

So, what can you do to minimize the possibility of a strike, walkout or riot? What can you do to minimize opposition while actively encouraging the quiet majority's positive and constructive attitude?

The answer is twofold: first, build up a good reputation for communicating to your employees at all times so that when difficulties emerge the process of communicating with them appears natural and credible and the style is familiar and reassuring.

Second, cultivate good relations with the local journalists – especially at times when you don't necessarily need them but when they might need your co-operation. Such scores count at important moments – although you'll never find a journalist who'll admit it.

This makes all the more important the flow of positive copy and the fiddling, time-consuming and sometimes irritating human interest story which is the life blood of the local media. Neglect it in good times at your peril; you never know when you might need its benefits.

The simple life

Neglect also the opportunities to do the simple, inexpensive things and you'll often find problems come home to roost. For example, any good plant or office manager spends time with their people – actually on the factory floor or in the general office. They make it a practice to 'walk the job' regularly, stopping to ask about a project or a difficulty or simply to pass the time of day.

To be seen is to become recognizable, familiar and therefore reassuring. It costs little in time and money and is the wisest investment you can make.

Fred on the assembly line is much less likely to take industrial action and much more likely to think that you care if you've just asked about his prize leeks at the Flower Show. It is partly this almost Victorian paternalism which has helped many of the successful magnates of British enterprise.

And do remember the notice board; it's not just there for pictures of Bruce Springsteen or Liverpool FC. It's there to let you say things to your employees and for them to become used to reading what you're saying. It's useful for standard notices like safety at work, office procedures, social events, fire drills and staff facilities, but it's also a way of subliminally selling more general underlying messages – and the more they read it, the more they believe it.

To retain its credibility, however, it must be kept up to date. Nothing looks worse than a notice advertising a function which happened last month. Updating and general tidiness should be the responsibility of a supervisor or foreman and their job will be simpler if you colour code your notices by month or week. That will also encourage readers to scan what's new more regularly and thus help to increase the board's usefulness as a communications tool.

It's also useful for specific campaigns: on quality or good housekeeping or energy saving. And it's there for that time honoured institution, the Suggestion Scheme. If this is to be successful it has to be heavily marketed and that means, among other things, that the prizes have to be tempting; otherwise people simply won't make the effort. So decide on the importance of it in your scheme of things and then budget to spend at least twice as much as you were going to. Include a Spanish holiday or a colour TV – the kind of prize that's worth a human interest story in the local paper. It all helps to boost the credit side of the media and employee balance.

The major influencers at home
The pay packet route is an example of how to use conventional personnel procedures to improve communications, especially to hourly paid employees. By inserting a message in the regular pay packet you can get straight to the psychological heart of the employee – the money he or she earns. The message becomes associated with rewards and all which that provides: home, food, warmth and so on. It graphically illustrates what a hasty action such as a strike vote may risk and what there is to be lost in terms of security – probably the most primitive but one of the strongest of the

basic needs and herd instincts still latently present in humans.

The pay packet message also has the advantage that it is often read by the employee's partner who is then able to add his or her opinion and balance the impetuous tendency of the workplace with the more stabilizing effect of the home. But use this device sparingly. Don't let it become intrusive or it will be self-defeating.

The role of the unions

Every month somewhere in British industry there is an object lesson of how *not* to treat the unions.

In communication terms there are still union officers who want to retain – or regain – the practice of talking to the employee instead of allowing management to do so because that is the only real way that they can exercise control over the workforce. Conversely if they allow you to communicate freely, then they perceive that you have it in your power to exercise the proper management authority. That seldom leaves an influential role for them.

Be careful therefore. The stakes may be higher than you imagined.

Treat union representatives civilly and properly; observe scrupulously the codes and practices of industrial relations and personnel procedures and stick to the letter of the law. Unions can only be powerfully destructive if you neglect one or all of these maxims and if you are not in close touch with your employees.

But above all, don't let anyone else do your communicating for you. You lose control of the hearts and minds of your employees. It's *your* responsibility. You're paid to lead a workforce, not to abrogate that responsibility to others not on your management team and not necessarily of your views.

Inform the conveners, stewards and even the local officials of your plans before you implement them; otherwise you may be in breach of an agreement. But do not give them the time to do anything about it. Don't let them speak at your meetings or pre-empt your information bulletin or employee letter with a broadsheet. Don't let them hold a mass meeting before you've given your presentation. And don't let them have the last word either. Make sure that your message is the one the employees take home.

The whole thing sounds like a rather petty political manoeuvre but, unfortunately, in some areas of industry and commerce, that's exactly what it still is. Therefore it has to be treated as such no matter what the company does or what size it is.

Finally, in talking to employees and to unions, remember Alice. 'Say what you mean and mean what you say.' And you'll find that, although communicating can sometimes resemble the bad dream of a Mad Hatter's Tea Party, the common sense of awakening can usually be achieved by hard, straight talking.

9 Employing a PR consultancy

As with most occupations, in PR there is an alternative to doing it yourself. The PR consultancy, while not a totally new phenomenon, has mushroomed over the last twenty-five years and now constitutes a thriving industry.

So, what are the advantages and disadvantages of using a PR consultancy? How do you go about choosing the right consultancy for your needs and, very importantly, how do you ensure that you are getting value for money once you have appointed your consultancy?

In order to answer these questions it is necessary to outline how consultancies are run and what they do.

PR consultancies
PR consultancies exist to help clients overcome specific communications difficulties and to provide a service of continuing advice and activity in the broad field of communications. Most clients first go to a consultancy when they have a problem of some sort and then continue the relationship as they see the need develop and the results justifying the expenditure. Relatively few clients retain a consultancy simply to improve the balance of their marketing mix, despite the fact that this is the area in which consultancies can often offer most.

Advertising without being supported by professionally devised and executed publicity programmes can often be akin to pouring money down the drain; it is here that consultancies can help a great deal. Indeed, media support may be the area in which many of them operate best – pulling down the media coverage to support the launch of a new product or to sustain the marketing effort behind a range of continuing offerings.

Most consultancies will attempt to diagnose the problem you are having in the first place and recommend the solutions. Naturally enough, these solutions will usually involve a fair amount of input from them, but that is the case with most consultants in most walks of life. There's not much point in having specialized knowledge unless you can make a living out of it.

If the consultancy is any good the initial diagnosis will consist of a series of sections roughly corresponding to these headings:

- *Objective*: setting out where you want to be at the end of the programme.
- *Strategy*: identifying broad means by which you are going to get there, including identifying any particular financial, political or logistical considerations which must be taken into account.
- *Key messages*: identifying positive aspects of your business, product and service which must be communicated.
- *Target audiences*: identifying those to whom your key messages need to be communicated.
- *Methodology*: describing the detail of how the work will be done in light of all the previous considerations and including a rough plan of the timing and expenditure of the work.
- *Financial implications*: a PR way of telling you what it will cost.

- *Timetable*: optional but usually included to frighten you to death about the timescale so that you will agree to work starting next week at a fee you can't afford.

There's nothing sacrosanct about this format, and it obviously differs from one consultancy to another, but most of the elements will be common even if they are called by some other name.

What will it cost you?

Consultancies earn their money in two main ways: *fees* which can be either a retaining or a project fee, and *commission* which is a handling or administrative charge levied on a piece of work.

Since you may be involved in spending relatively large sums of money, it is worth looking at these categories in more detail.

The fee

Most consultancies will try to convince you that the programme of activity which you need cannot be achieved in a couple of months and, therefore, you need a longer term relationship. They are usually right. This relationship is based upon a given programme of work which is devised by the consultancy and agreed, or amended, by you, the client. Once agreed, it is finally costed on the basis of the time that it will take the consultancy to put into practice the agreed activities. (A rough costing may have been worked out earlier to guide you.)

This consultancy time is charged out at varying rates depending on the seniority and experience of the person or people who are working on your business. Senior executives clearly charge higher fees than juniors and the whole – and often complicated equation – is worked out to a total fee over a given period, usually one year. A total budget is then put to you on this basis and the fee divided into convenient parts or instalments, usually monthly.

The upshot of this is that you are faced with a monthly fee which is usually paid in advance in order to retain the time and expertise of the people involved from the consultancy.

If your requirement is essentially short term (a product launch, perhaps, or a series of sequential events such as a festival), there is clearly a limited timescale in which the work must be done and, in these circumstances, a project fee will be suggested which will cover not just the event itself (by which time any work the consultancy will do will probably be too late), but also the run-up period, which is seldom less than three months, and, because of lead times in the publishing world, should usually be at least six months. Generally, 50 per cent of this fee is invoiced in advance, and the other 50 per cent upon the successful completion of the programme.

In either case, if the work turns out to be significantly more than was agreed, the consultancy will often ask for a further fee to cover the extra time which is being taken. This can lead to interesting debates: is extra time being spent because the original requirements have changed or because the consultancy is undertaking more work than was originally envisaged? If the latter, did you receive notice of it in writing before this extra work was started and did you then agree to this extra expenditure, also in writing, or did it just happen?

Furthermore, it is possible that the consultancy finds that, once the work is underway, it is taking longer than was planned, especially at senior level. This may be difficult for the consultancy, but that does not mean that you should have to pay any extra money. What it means is that the consultancy should plan its work and its budgets on a more professional basis.

It could even be that the consultancy is requesting more money because it has been unable to satisfactorily achieve your original objectives. Have nothing to do with this. Provided the brief which you supplied was clear, the consultancy's plans were sensible, professional and agreed by you at the outset and the fee adequate, there is no reason why you should be paying more money to reward lack of achievement.

There are a few golden rules about using a PR consultancy. The very first one is to make sure you agree in advance exactly what the fee covers, exactly how much you will have to pay and exactly when you will have to pay it. It is not that there are more rogues in PR consultancies than anywhere else; it is just that the profession is so young that codes of practice, while admirable, are not yet as binding or as widely adhered to as they are in, say, law or accountancy.

Moreover, the methods of business differ considerably from one consultancy to another and large outfits in particular tend to follow their big brothers in advertising in the way in which they structure their business and their fees.

One useful safeguard is to choose only those consultancies which are members of the Public Relations Consultants' Association (PRCA), an industry body which acts as a setter of standards and a watchdog, among other activities. Most self-respecting consultancies belong to it and, although it is not an independent body in that its members are taken from the very consultancies they represent, it does offer some redress and means of arbitration should the need arise.

Commission

Levying a handling charge is very much an advertising agency practice which has crept into many consultancies as they have either been taken over by advertising agencies or as they have become more commercially aware.

Simply put, and it is not a simple process, it involves the consultancy placing a charge on any work which it purchases on the client's behalf. If the client has agreed the need for a brochure, for example, the consultancy will brief a graphic designer (a process which should be covered in the original fee, but is sometimes charged as a separate expense) and commission designs for the client to assess. When one is chosen, it will go through to the artwork stage so that the printer can work from it and the designer then invoices the consultancy – not the client – for the work done.

The consultancy pays – provided both it and the client are happy with the work – and then invoices the client for the design work plus a management or handling charge which can vary enormously. The industry norm is 17.65 per cent, a bizarre figure arrived at by adding 15 per cent commission and then 15 per cent of the 15 per cent commission to cover VAT. However, greater commissions are not unknown and all bills which a PR consultancy sends through over and above the fee are, therefore, worth close examination.

To return to the brochure and the commission that can mount up. Once the artwork is made, the copy has to be written and photographs or other illustrations may have to be created. This is something else the consultancy can do for you, and will usually suggest. Copywriting, however, is something few consultancies are happy to keep in house, often because their staff are so stretched that they spend all their time keeping clients happy and presenting somebody else's work. Consequently, copywriting is a service which is regularly bought in. So the consultancy gets somebody else to do the work while still taking a commission for managing it.

Photography is another service which is often bought in by the consultancy and allows another opportunity to add commission. The same rule applies to processing and typesetting so that, by the time the brochure arrives at the printers, it has already cost the client a fair amount of money.

Printers' fees, already high, are less likely to attract a commission when passed on to the client, partly because the mark up is going to be so much more obvious. A print bill of £10,000 (by no means uncommon) looks considerably worse with another £1,765 added on.

So, at the end of the day, the brochure has cost quite a lot of money, certainly 15 per cent more than it would have done had the client done it himself and, because the extra is added at every stage and at varying levels, probably considerably more than that. In return, the client has had the co-ordination and liaison work done and that is not a job which is to be taken lightly. There are undoubted skills in making a project like a brochure come together at the right time and to the right budget.

In your case, it may be that you are perfectly happy to pay someone to oversee this activity, especially if your knowledge of printing, writing, design, layout and illustration is pretty basic. An expert oversees a specialized exercise – and that service has its price. Whether its price is equal to 15 per cent or more of the total is up to you to decide. Whatever you decide, it is always worth asking to see the original bills from the suppliers to the consultancy, if only to hear the various excuses when this request is refused, as it usually is.

Value for money
There is no doubt that some clients pay some consultancies far more than they should and do not receive anything like value for their money. On the other hand, this argument has been levelled at such pillars of society as estate agents and solicitors for many years without any noticeable improvement in the standard of service. Taken as a whole, PR consultancies are probably no worse than anyone else in this respect, but they are probably no better either.

For example, a consultancy undertook an assignment for a foreign government two or three years ago. The job lasted only a week but involved a heavy schedule of following an overseas diplomat around the South East all day and every day recording his activities and speeches on video. At three o'clock every afternoon, the whole of the previous twenty-four hours' worth of coverage was couriered back to London, edited down to a digest of between five and fifteen minutes and at six o'clock bounced off a satellite to New York for onward transmission to the client country.

This exercise involved outlay from the consultancy both in time and cash: partly because video companies and satellites have to be booked and paid for in advance and partly because it was a demanding schedule that required experienced and continuous handling. In the event it was a great success. All the broadcasts went out on time and a few photographs and transcripts of speeches and other UK coverage were added as well.

For the whole of the week's work, the consultancy charged a fee of £7,000 which was, probably, reasonable. On top of that, it incurred total outgoings of around £8,000 to pay for the video company, the satellite slots and other necessary expenditure. However, in invoicing this latter cost, the sum changed from £8,000 to £15,000, thus making a total income of £22,000 against an outgoing of £8,000 and effectively doubling the fee. £14,000 profit isn't bad for one week's work, especially as it was less than full-time work in that the consultancy team kept on working for other clients at the same time.

Profits are all very well (and very necessary in any business), but this kind of petty minded and cynical approach betrays at least two shortcomings.

It demonstrates a flagrant disregard for the ethics of the business and it shows a singularly myopic and naive approach to the prospect of gaining further work from the client concerned. Nobody in their right minds would pay £22,000 for a week's work when it was pretty obvious that the market value was considerably below that. As far as I know the consultancy in question never won any further business from that client which, under the circumstances, is hardly surprisingly.

This example raises a further interesting question – that of the structure of a consultancy; how could decisions like this be made without alienating the majority of staff who are honest and conscientious?

Structure and organization

Consultancies come in three sizes: large, small and don't knows. All have in common the fact that they were founded by an individual or a small group of people who were well versed in various aspects of PR. Not surprisingly, the consultancies have tended to develop as reflections of this original expertise so that they still specialize in the strengths of the founders. Thus, there are consultancies which deal predominantly with financial affairs or political activities, food and drink or sponsorship, business advice or fast moving consumer goods activity.

Whatever the speciality, the consultancies share also the effects of having been created recently in a growth industry: autocratic management and feudal structures, under-resourcing and indifferent cash flow, lack of investment and very high staff turnover.

Something else many of them share is that they have developed their business to a size which is no longer comfortable as a one or two person band, but which is not properly organized as a company – a sort of uneasy half-way house.

A typical structure in a large or medium-sized consultancy resembles that of an Anglo-Saxon feudal manor:

Chairman
|
Chief Executive or Managing Director
|
Board Directors
|
Associate Directors
|
Account Directors

|

Account Managers

|

Senior Account Executives

|

Account Executives

|

Junior Account Executives

|

Account Assistants

|

Graduate Trainees

Such a structure would not be out of place in ICI or BP let alone A. N. Other PR Ltd but it is remarkably prevalent and is explained by a number of factors.

One is the staff problem. The business has grown like topsy and, in the process, most of the available talent has long since found a niche or started up on its own. Therefore, any staff have to be well looked after, offered considerable inducements just to join and even more to stay. There is a headhunting carousel in the PR consultancy world, in London at least, which keeps quite a number of headhunters in very comfortable employment. Virtually all the big consultancies are perpetually on the look out for good people, to a degree that would be unthinkable in the older established professions that have had the benefit of decades, if not centuries, of training to bring on young professionals.

At the same time, PR consultancies are not noted for their profitability. One sizable firm which was taken over a couple of years ago was trading at less than 5 per cent profit margin and this is by no means unusual. Consequently, inducements to staff sometimes have to take the form of prestige rather than cash. An Account Director may only be paid £20,000–£30,000 but is called a director at an early age – mid-twenties is not uncommon. Similarly, the various account handlers may change jobs for very little more money but an extra title. It's the sort of incremental differentiation which the Ford Motor Company perceived and turned to advantage years ago by branding externally very similar cars in a socially graded manner: L, GL, GLS and Ghia. The difference is that very few self-respecting PR consultants would be seen dead in a Sierra, even taking into account the fact that few consultancies offer cars to title holders below Director.

Another reason for the feudalism is simply the fact that the founder, who probably insists on keeping his name in the company title, often cannot bear to let go of the little outfit he founded a decade or more before. Consequently, the structure is designed to discourage real power sharing while promoting the concept of industrial democracy and shared benefits – double speak of no small proportions.

Very few good PR people are also good business people. Indeed, it sometimes seems that the two qualities are mutually exclusive. Whatever the reason, very few consultancies are really run as soundly based and structured businesses until they're either taken over by a proper business or until the founders have the sense to involve business people who are not PR people to keep the thing on the rails.

This may seem irrelevant to you until you come to decide on appointing a PR consultancy, but then the consequences of its past become apparent and can have a major effect on the way in which your two companies interact.

The appointment

Assuming that you've firmly decided to appoint a PR consultancy, the first stage is to draw up a shortlist of those consultancies which you think may fit your bill. One of the first considerations (and it is essential that you have this clearly in your mind before you even brief somebody) is what, exactly, you want that consultancy to do on your behalf. Without establishing the ground rules early on in the relationship, neither you nor the consultancy will benefit from the contract. Do you, for instance, want a media relations job, an internal communications job or a higher business profile? Do you really know what you want or are you merely aware of a vague need, the satisfying of which would in some way improve your business?

If you are not sure, seek expert advice. You could go to a PR consultancy for this advice of course, but, since very few are equipped to act as genuine management consultants, you are probably better off spending an evening taking a long hard look at the way in which you think your company is perceived, how your products, services, staff and activities are regarded and what is your standing in the marketplace you have chosen. From there it should be possible to identify the areas of weakness. You might be well known in your home town, for example, but not in a town twenty miles away. You may have identified an export opportunity, but be unaware of the preparatory stages necessary to put it into practice. You may have a new product launch coming up which could transform the whole of your business, but be unsure about how best to launch it, where, when and to whom.

Once you've decided what sort of PR service you need the next stage is to research those consultancies which you wish to look at. This is the point at which many clients go wrong. They neglect the important research stage and find themselves lumbered with an expensive and not wholly relevant overhead for quite some time. Information on PR consultancies is not readily available unless you know where to look but it can be obtained. The IPR and the PRCA will both be pleased to offer advice and there are now a few consultancy brokers who will research the best solutions for your problems, write briefs, draw up shortlists and assist in the selection process.

As a general rule, try to pick a consultancy whose management style closely fits your own. Some will try to run your account as though they were running your business which easily leads to friction. Some may only work certain office hours that don't fit in with yours; some may have very firm preconceived ideas about what they can give you – as opposed to what you need. Some may disagree with what you're doing. Tobacco companies, for example, have found difficulty in this area during the last few years.

Above all, pick on a consultancy your own size. Big is not necessarily beautiful in the PR world and the large consultancies have a marked preference for big accounts. Even a consultancy at the bottom end of the Top Twenty will probably not be interested in accounts involving a fee retainer of less than £40,000 a year; and £3,000 a month is a lot to spend merely to retain someone's skills and pay the rental on their BMW.

Moreover, large consultancies are continually hard pressed to meet their business commitments. The staffing problem has reached such a stage that only the most essential tasks can be performed and client contact is, in the eyes of some consultancies, a relative luxury to be kept for occasions of absolute necessity.

It is far better, especially if you're a small business, to go for a small or medium-sized consultancy where you are more sure of receiving the personal attention that you deserve and for which you pay. Indeed, personal attention is all in a PR consultancy, even more so than it is in other consultancies, and it is essential that you choose a good operator with whom you get on, with whom you have similar opinions and with whom you share a common vision of the future of your business.

Furthermore, smaller consultancies are not necessarily less expensive but certainly better value for money to the small client. You and the consultancy account team get to know each other more quickly, there is a more rapid learning curve and, usually, a greater commitment to your account because it is one of only two or three upon which a consultant works rather than one of a dozen.

A Board Director of a sizable PR consultancy will run a group of about twenty accounts, most of them from a wide variety of business backgrounds and all of them rightly demanding a presence and input from that director. This is a very difficult position to maintain. Not only is it virtually impossible to keep track of the various developments in all the different industry sectors, it is also difficult to get to know the influential press very well or to spend time on the more remote offshoots of the main client – areas which often need more attention than they receive.

It is some consolation to have a number of good people working in the group, but the downside of this is that the director inevitably and irrevocably loses immediacy, contact and involvement with the account. He or she could as well be a director of a steamed pudding factory for all the relevance PR has to the task in hand. Most of the time is taken up in personnel, finance and general management matters (as it would be in any other directorship in any other discipline), and that is not something for which most clients are prepared to pay fat fees.

Once you've decided on the shortlist (keep it down to three or you'll waste a lot of time and money), prepare a brief and check that the chosen few do not have conflicting business, that is, that they do not handle the account of one of your competitors. If they do, they will almost certainly pull out of the pitch, unless your account looks like being a better bet – that is, becoming more profitable.

After that, two meetings should be enough to make up your mind: one to issue the brief, discuss it and find out something about the consultancy that your research has not yielded (what the people are like, for example) and the second meeting to receive the proposals.

These will usually be formally 'presented', either on overhead slide, flip chart or, if you've really got a plum account, 35 mm slide. Accompanying them should be a 'leave-behind' document, a book of the film which you can take away and digest in coming to your decision. This is often more revealing than the presentation itself and it is important that you meet the author of this screed at the presentation.

Crucial also is that the people who are making the presentation to you are those who will work on your business should you decide to appoint this consultancy. Too often, consultancies, especially large ones, send in the heavy guns to gain business and then have lunch with you – at your ultimate expense – every six months or so.

Insist, therefore, on seeing a chart of the account team and ensure that the star presenter is both on it as your account director, and that he or she is a real live account handler who will be busying himself or herself with your business on a day-to-day basis, including writing copy for you. Ensure also that your account director is available to see you at least once a month for a reasonable period of time. If he or she is not, then you probably need to look elsewhere for your service.

Beware also of the high powered senior PR director who fronts the presentation, swears he will head up your account and then fulfils this promise by reading your press cuttings once a month. Ask how many other accounts he heads up. If it's more than three, he hasn't got time to take up a true hands-on role on your business as well.

Cost-effectiveness
The measurement of how effective your PR consultancy is – or is not – can only come from its impact on your overall business. How much more widely are you known, how much more appreciated are your services, how much in demand are your goods, how well respected are your staff?

Yet, these are not easily quantifiable measurements and, even at their best, can be intangible.

Some clients, and consultancies too, resort to the old column inches test: a monthly compendium of all the press cuttings achieved by the product, brand or service is presented to the Board in order to justify the consultancy's existence. Unfortunately, many other factors can affect this measurement and the argument that your PR consultancy is worth £X because that is the advertising value of the space occupied by the press cuttings is nullified by the fact that you might not be advertising in those media anyway. Also, it only takes a big enough negative story about your business to get into the media and you could find yourself awash with column inches, none of which you wanted. There are times when PR consultancies should be (and are) paid on what is not printed rather then what is.

The real test of the PR consultancy's effectiveness must come from within you, the client.

- Do you feel that it is doing your business any good?
- Are you achieving targets that you might not otherwise have achieved?
- Are your staff and your dealers more contented and more motivated as a result of greater communication?
- Is the climate in which you operate your business more conducive to your success?
- Are you extending the range of influential contacts which may be necessary to put into practice the next stage of your development plan?
- Are you, and is your business, product or service, any more widely known now than it was before you appointed a PR consultancy?
- Above all, do you get the service that you need at a price that is fair?

Only you can answer these questions.

Consultancy versus in-house

Looking at the issue from another perspective, what can a consultancy achieve that an in-house PR operation cannot? The answer here is complex and depends to a great extent on the nature and size of your business. To a small business, the overhead of even one, reasonable PR person is quite a lot of money: say, £25,000 minimum when salary, car, insurance and pension have all been taken into account. Then there are overhead costs: office, secretary, heat, light, rates and so on. Finally, there are the operating costs: printing, postage, telephone, travel, subsistence, entertainment, photography, seminars, exhibitions, conferences, literature, giveaways and so on. The list can become almost endless.

If you take the amount of fixed overhead and do not exceed its equivalent in the fees you pay the PR consultancy, then you are probably going to show a minor cash saving. But that in itself does not mean that you have secured a better deal. In-house operations can be more loyal than consultancies and they certainly devote more of their time and effort to your business. They may be less experienced, initially at least, but that can soon be remedied.

The consultancy has access to greater resources, should you have need of them, and can bring to bear big guns which you cannot afford – and would not wish to afford – to carry on your own payroll. Good media contacts, for instance, should be part of all consultancies' armoury. But, you can always hire in this kind of help for the big occasions (such as product launches) without having to retain it all the time.

And here, probably, lies the secret of success in handling your PR affairs. Do the daily, routine stuff in-house with a member of staff who may have other responsibilities as well; bring in the consultancy for the big events which require experience and stage management, but do not put them on a retainer; pay them a project fee worked out on a time basis. That way, they will not become stale or complacent; they will not stop trying to achieve – and that is something that too many PR consultants do once they've got the contract signed and the fee in the bank.

Above all, have an idea firmly fixed in your mind of what you want your consultancy to achieve. Brief it accordingly, amend and agree the approach through the various stages of strategy and methodology, agree a financial limit within which it has relative freedom but beyond which it will not go, and, finally, monitor its work and its progress regularly. No consultancy really likes being left alone altogether, although most prefer that to constant interference.

Insist on regular meetings (at least once a fortnight and preferably once a week). In order to meet regularly, ensure that you've made the commitment in time and effort as well as in money. Ensure also that the consultancy has free access to your business facts and figures and the broader basis of your industry knowledge. Without that advantage, it will have to spend a good deal of your money re-inventing the wheel by learning about things which you may know off by heart – clearly not a profitable use of its time or your money.

At your regular meetings, or in advance of them, the consultancy should produce a contact report. This, without becoming a series of long-winded minutes, briefly records all decisions which have been reached between you, especially any referring to money and policy. These reports will build up into a useful reference base which you can glance over at the end of the year to refresh your memory about what has been done and how well it has been achieved. It should be a useful aide memoire when it comes to deciding on the following year's budget.

Compare the achievements also with the original and updated plans which have been submitted by the consultancy to ensure that they are good at delivering what they promise and propose as well as at producing fancy sounding words and concepts. There is an art in writing plans and proposals which can seduce even the most hard headed client and this art is almost as widespread in PR consultancies as it is in advertising agencies.

At the end of the day, you want to see real results for your money, not just long documents or quasi-academic matrices. For this, your own business instinct is the best guide in your search for value for money.

10 Starting up

So, you are ready to embark upon some form of PR activity to support aspects of your business. How are you going to go about it? What preparations do you need to make? How will you plan your work and your expenditure? What short-term targets should you set and how will you see these gradually turn into longer term landmarks?

The key to really successful PR lies, as in so many other tasks, in *planning*. Everything you do should be premeditated. Some of it necessarily won't be because that's the way that PR works some of the time, but the more tightly you plan, the greater rewards you will derive from your expenditure.

Begin by putting down on paper what your problems are in the area you want to address. Be totally honest with yourself otherwise there's no point in the exercise. Set out what you need to improve in PR terms: your product, company or personal reputation perhaps, or the awareness of your service.

Then look at the people, dealers, newspapers, magazines, official bodies and all other forms of catalyst who have it in their power to influence the problems and reputations you have identified, either for better or for worse.

Next, set out all the messages that could be given to these catalysts that will encourage them to make efforts to improve the situation: your strengths, achievements, plans and investments for the future.

Then jot down as many ways as you can think of by which you could bring these two elements together: how to get the message to the catalyst. Don't bother to formalize it too much yet, just jot down ideas as fast as they flow from your pen.

Then take each idea in turn and subject it to a long hard critical appraisal. Is it possible? Could you do it? Have you got the time and the skills? If not, can you afford to pay somebody who has?

Have you got enough good ideas or do you need to enlist the help of somebody to whom this kind of work is more familiar? Do you think you can write well enough to construct a decent press release for instance? (Most journalists will tell you that many professional PR people cannot write very well, anyway, so why not have a go?)

Have you got time to devote to building relationships with the media, or the dealers, or all the other bodies whose help you are going to need? If not, can you find the time by delegating some of your other duties? Or is there anyone else in your organization who has the time and the ability to act in a media relations role?

What sort of timescale is realistic for achieving the ideas that you've put down? Can they be done in time to affect your business for this year or should they be budgeted for next year?

How exactly are these ideas going to be put into practice? Do you know the detail of what's to be done? If not, who do you know who does and who will be willing to help?

Once you've got enough workable ideas down on paper, look to see how they fit in with whatever else is going to be happening in your business in the foreseeable future: new product launches, moves to new premises, the introduction of new services, the recruiting of new employees, investment in new processes. All these can greatly help your PR programme and can, in turn, be greatly helped by it.

Having got to this stage, try to conceptualize all this into a schedule of activity for, say, the next six months. (Remember though that many periodicals have lead times of three months or more.) Try to plan your PR activity so that it forms a consistent flow of stories, activities and initiatives rather than being all bunched up together. Try to achieve an even spread of news so that your target audiences get used to the idea of regular communication and begin to approach you as someone worth talking to.

You'll end up with a wall planner full of activities and dates and plans. You'll also by then have some idea of how they are – or are not – going to happen.

Only at this stage should you consider the financial aspects of what you're thinking about doing. You know whether you can afford to carry out certain plans of action; by the same token, only you know whether you can afford not to carry them out. The decision must be taken at this stage whether or not to go ahead on the merits of what you have worked out, the probable effect on your public profile and the consequent impact on your business.

Once you've balanced the actions and the expenditure, then is the time to decide further about involving other people and, specifically, PR consultancies. Even if you do use one, this planning process is still useful – perhaps even more so. You can then measure their thinking and performance against what you know to be roughly the right blend of activity. If they get somewhere near your conclusions, then you're probably all thinking on the same lines and these are more likely to be the right ones.

When you've decided what to do, and with whom, draw up a special PR budget. Make sure it is included in your overall financial plan, in just the same way that the PR programme must be made to fit into the aims and strategies of your overall business plan. Only by fully integrating both these areas will you ever be able to maximize the benefits of PR to your business.

Carrying out the plan

Planning is one thing; carrying out these plans is another exercise entirely. As with other activities, unless you force yourself to regard PR as an important discipline to which you must allocate a realistic proportion of your time, then it will not happen properly and your business will not show the benefits of a well-executed PR programme.

Too often, PR programmes suffer because they are seen as desirable rather than necessary and, when resources and time run short, they are among the first to be cut. It is at exactly this sort of time that the PR programme more than comes into its own. It can persuade an otherwise sceptical world that your business is on a sound footing when the withdrawing of an advertising programme will serve only to deepen suspicions about your profitability or cash flow. It can instil a sense of confidence by telling the truth about a product safety issue while a resounding silence only serves to heighten righteous indignation and militant consumerism.

Some Japanese companies have a rule known as 'The 75 Day Event'. In a nutshell, this regards any major PR difficulty as a 75 day wonder, the publicity mileage of which will have been exhausted after this period has elapsed.

Well, this may be so in Japan, but if it is, it shows the Japanese press as being very much less inquisitive than Western press. If 75 days were so important, President Nixon and John Profumo could both have enjoyed rather more dignified ends to their careers.

PR is a very necessary discipline and not just in a defensive or reactionary mode. It is a valid and formidable marketing tool and, as such, needs to be accorded at least as much

weight and vigour as advertising and promotion. Consequently, it needs to be planned and followed through with
equal vigour.

How best is this done? In a small company, personal
service is all. Have a go yourself in the first instance. It may
not work very well to start with, but you will soon get the
hang of it. You will discover that much of it is commonsense
and customer courtesy, and find not only that it works but
that it also leads to further opportunities.

At the very least, you will discover what your PR
difficulties really are, and that in itself will stand you in very
good stead if you decide that you need to recruit or retain a
professional to continue the work. You will not only know
what needs to be done; but you will also have an idea of how
it should be done. This makes progress monitoring and
performance assessment easier than it would be from a
position of total ignorance.

Bear in mind also that PR can contribute to many more
disciplines than merely marketing. It can directly contribute
to the personnel function through employee relations skills
and programmes. It can assist the finance function by
directing the thoughts of notoriously unliterary staff and
explaining and presenting them to audiences both inside and
outside the company. It can help the training of all kinds of
manufacturing and production staff by presenting training
modules in terms which the trainees understand and can
relate to. It can greatly assist the bottom line sales effort by
creating a climate of opinion favourable to clinching the sale.
And it can act as an intelligence gatherer and path smoother
for the planning function.

By the success of all these functions must the success of
the PR function be judged. It is a true staff function as well as
being the line function at the very sharpest edge of the coal
face. It is a rare combination of responsibilities and one
which takes a great deal of strain if properly used.

Accordingly, it acquires and retains a sense of independence from the mainstream of the company's structure. It is not, and should not be, part of the Marketing Department. It is a truly inter-departmental discipline and one which must always retain its integrity in this way if it is to carry out its work properly.

As a function, it sits on the Board, has access to the Chairman and all other senior managers at all times, every day if necessary. It is represented at all policy decision making processes so that it can adequately represent the company at all external – and some internal – functions.

In this way it is truly integrated, but maintains a true integrity. It compliments and complements at the same time. It makes or breaks reputations – and companies. Furthermore, it's quite good fun. Have a go and find out for yourself.

Index